THE WORLD'S BEST

STREET
FOOD

WHERE TO FIND IT
& HOW TO MAKE IT

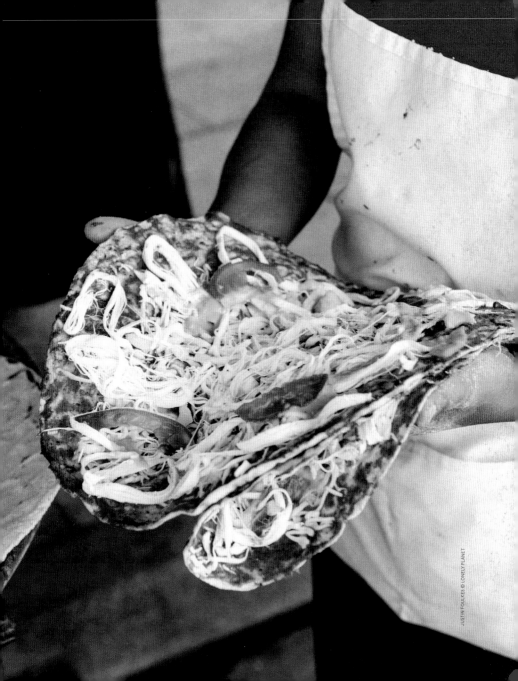

CONTENTS

INTRODUCTION

BY TOM PARKER BOWLES

You never forget the first time. Mine took place, nearly 20 years back, on an insalubrious backstreet in Bangkok's Patpong. The experience was brief, and fairly inglorious, but remains seared in my soul forever. One taste was all it took. The stall was little more than a pushcart with a bright yellow awning. A tattered advert for Carnation milk hung precariously from the side while the owner, a small woman in a Coca-Cola cap, gossiped incessantly with a friend perched on a wobbly plastic stool. Workspace was severely limited, as a huge wooden pestle and mortar dominated

the display. Neatly arranged around it, like small satellites circling the sun, were metal bowls filled with ingredients of every hue.

As a street-food virgin, I wasn't exactly sure where to start. A friend more experienced in the ways of the road had told me about *som tam*. 'Just look for the stall with the fat, shiny green fruit. And someone pounding the hell out of their mortar.' So I giggled nervously and pointed at the plump papaya. The lady stopped her chat and smiled back. 'You want *farang* hot? Or Thai hot?' she asked as she threw a handful of green beans into the dark wooden depths. 'Umm, Thai hot,' I muttered, puffing out my chest. 'OK,' she answered, adding what seemed like a suicidal amount of scud chillies, along with a few cloves of garlic. She pounded and mixed with a technique well honed by experience. I was mesmerised. Dried shrimp and peanuts were dropped in. Pound, pound, mix, mix, mix. Then palm sugar and tomatoes. Pound, pound, mix, mix. And lime juice and fish sauce. Pound, pound, mix. Then a mass of green papaya, cut into the thinnest of strands. One final mix, and it was dumped onto a polystyrene tray and handed over.

I took a bite. The first taste was sharp and fresh, then salty, from the chewy dried shrimp. Sweetness came next, underscoring and smoothing every discordant note. Tomatoes jostled with peanuts and crisp green beans as they swirled around my mouth. An involuntary smile spread across my face. This was food like I'd never tasted before, big, ballsy and beautifully balanced, the sort of thing to restore one's faith in life, love, the universe...then the chillies hit. Hard. So hard that my eyes flooded with tears, my tongue seemed to swell and I lost the power of speech. Even thinking hurt.

MATT MUNRO © LONELY PLANET IMAGES. © TIM E WHITE

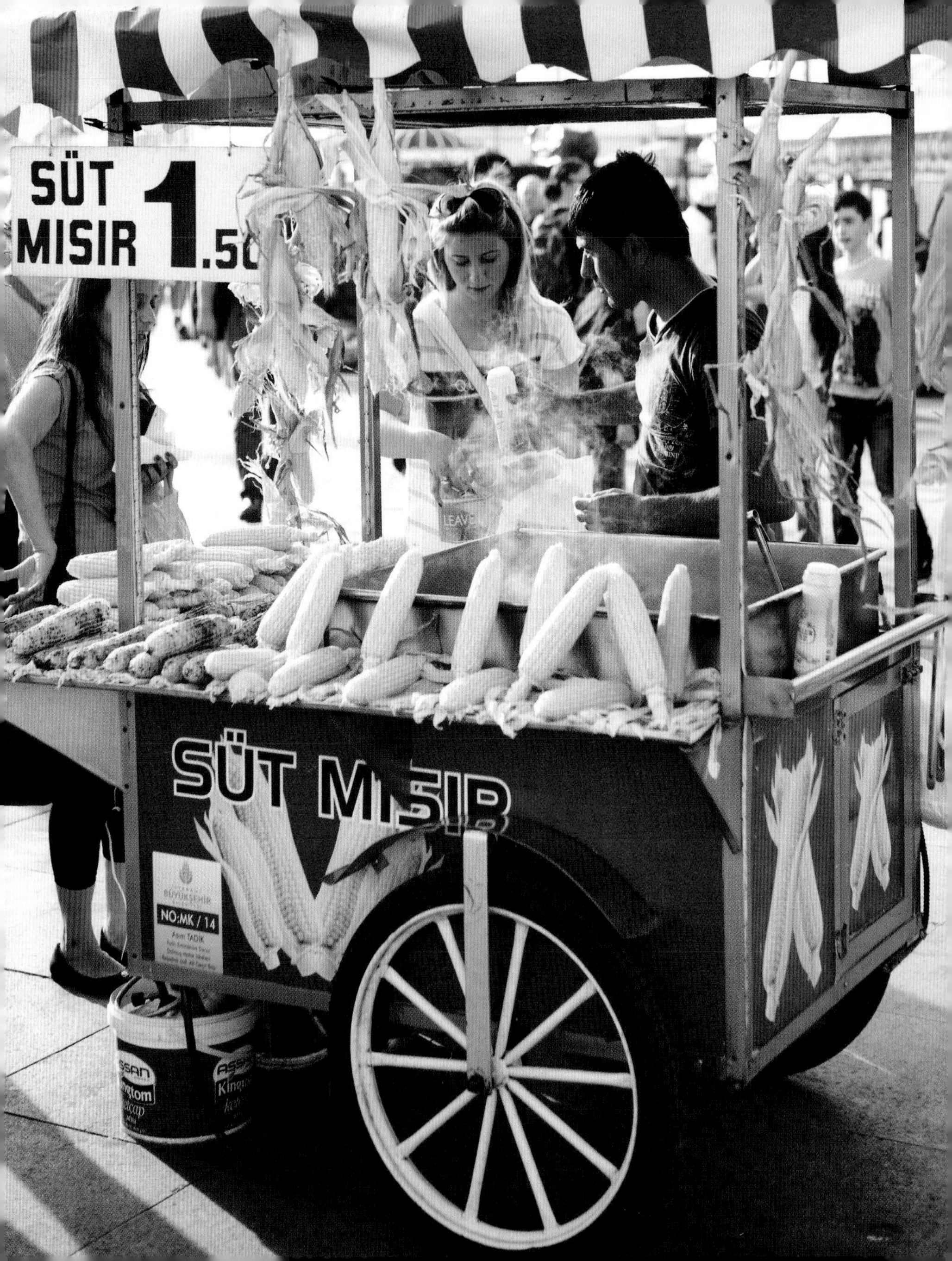
SÜT
MISIR
1.50
SÜT MISIR
NO:MK / 14

It took a full five minutes for the pain to subside, replaced by that heady endorphin warmth sent in by the body to battle the pain. I looked up. Both ladies were crying. But tears of laughter rather than agony. 'You like?' asked one, between fits of hysterics. 'Yes,' I managed to mutter. 'Hell yes.'

Since then, street food has become my obsession. Some travel to drink in the culture, others to lap up the sun. I travel to eat, preferably on the street. Because this is where you'll find the real soul of a cuisine, somewhere among the taco carts and noodle stalls and baskets of herbs. Michelin stars hold little interest, with the rarest of exceptions. And the tourist restaurants, with their bland, dreary, 'safe' menus fill me with gloom. No, my first stop is always the street. The scent of wood fires and burning fat, the glare of artificial lights, the natural hubbub of regalement, and proper good cheer. No foams, or smears or strangely shaped plates. No egos, or supercilious sommeliers or dining rooms with all the atmosphere of a morgue. Just food to make the taste buds sing. Some of the finest things to ever have passed my lips have been eaten standing up, or sitting at the most rickety of roadside tables, surrounded by diesel fumes, cigarette smoke and noise. There was that noodle soup in Luang Prabang, the buffalo broth looking like melted amber, with a depth I can only dream of re-creating. Or those tacos al pastor from the hole in the wall in Mexico City – thin shavings of pork doner kebab, mixed with hot sauce, and fresh salsa, and lime. Then wrapped in a steaming taco. Baozi (Chinese steamed buns) in Shanghai, oyster cakes in Bangkok and panelle (chickpea-flour fritters), all soft, salty crunch, sold on a Palermo street corner. I could go on and on and on. Street food is the most democratic grub in the world, a place where politician eats alongside peasant, and flavours are unashamedly bold. I like the fact that countries with a strong street-food culture – Mexico, Thailand, China, Malaysia and Vietnam, to name but a few – take it very seriously indeed. Everyone has their own view as to what makes the finest tamales, samosas, stinky tofu, laksa or spring rolls.

That's not to say that everything cooked up on the sidewalk is edible gold. Far from it. There's a lot of tired, dirty, grease-soaked muck about. But that's easily avoided: local recommendations are worth their weight in spice, and always look for queues. High turnover not only means they must be getting something right, but that the food's cooked fresh too, as there isn't time for it to sit around. Find a busy stall, watch what the locals are ordering and when you arrive at the front, just smile and point. The only phrase you really need is 'thank you'.

This is a book dedicated to some of the greatest eating in the world. Gastronomic bliss awaits.

SAVOURY

In which we explore the whole gamut of tangy, piquant and downright delicious morsels the world's streets have to offer. From juicy dumplings and buttery lobster to crispy pastries stuffed with fragrant spices, the flavours of the planet's best roadside stalls and hawker markets are coming direct to your kitchen. →

ORIGINS

Acarajé was brought to Brazil by Yoruba-speaking slaves from West Africa, where bean fritters known as *akará* were (and continue to be) a staple. In the New World, *acarajé* evolved into a sacred food, associated with the Afro-Brazilian religion Candomblé and featuring in ritual meals offered to Lansã, goddess of fire, wind, thunder and lightning. Women from the sisterhood of Lansã became the first *acarajé* vendors, their presence in the streets dating back to the 19th century.

SALVADOR, BAHIA, BRAZIL

ACARAJÉ

A tantalising taste of Africa in the New World, these shrimp-stuffed black-eyed pea fritters fried in traditional Bahian *dendê* (reddish palm oil) are Brazil's most beloved street food.

YOU'LL NEED

400g (14oz) dried black-eyed
  peas, soaked overnight in
  plenty of cold water
1 onion, roughly chopped
1 tsp salt
dendê oil for deep-frying
dried shrimp
hot pepper sauce and
  chopped green tomatoes
  to serve

TIP *Using dendê oil will give
the fritters their characteristic
red hue, but if you do not
have a Brazilian grocer handy,
vegetable or canola oil is an
acceptable substitute.*

METHOD

1 Skin the peas by rubbing and breaking them up or by quickly pulsing in a food processor, resoaking in water and letting the loosened skins come up to the surface.

2 Discard the skins and drain the peas.

3 Using a food processor, puree the peas with the onion and salt into a smooth mixture.

4 Divide the mixture into equal size balls and flatten each ball into the shape of a hamburger patty.

5 Heat the oil in a deep-fryer or heavy-bottomed saucepan.

6 Fry each patty until it becomes golden brown in colour on both sides.

7 Slit each patty horizontally and fill the acarajé sandwich with dried shrimp, pepper sauce and green tomatoes. Serve immediately.

TASTING NOTES

Acarajé is sold on street corners throughout Bahia, but especially in Salvador. The traditional carts are operated by *baianas de acarajé*, women clad in the white hooped skirts and headscarves associated with Candomblé priestesses. The fun part is choosing the fillings: spicy *malagueta* sauce, dried shrimp, *vatapá* (a nut, coconut and shrimp paste), *salada* (tomatoes, onions and coriander) and *carurú* (a shrimp-and-okra stew). Crispy, pungent and spicy, it's a combination of tastes you won't encounter anywhere else. ● *by Gregor Clark*

YOU'LL NEED

For the rice mix
500g (1lb) arborio rice
salt
1 sachet saffron powder (0.1g)
3 egg yolks
100g (¼lb) grated pecorino or
 parmesan cheese
30g (1oz) butter

For the ragù filling
½ onion, finely chopped
1 tbs butter
olive oil
150g (5oz) mince (beef, pork
 or a mixture of both)
½ cup red wine
2 tbs tomato paste
salt
pepper
80g (2½oz) peas (fresh
 or frozen)

For assembly and frying
100g (¼lb) provola,
 caciocavallo or mozzarella
 cheese, cut into cubes
2 eggs, beaten
breadcrumbs
peanut or olive oil

ORIGINS

The *arancino* or 'little orange'
has its origins in the Arabic
cuisine that Sicily's 9th- and
10th-century Saracen rulers
brought with them from North
Africa. However, it wasn't until
the 13th century that chefs
started coating rice balls with
breadcrumbs and frying them,
the idea being to conserve the
rice and provide King Federico
II with a portable snack for his
hunting trips. Ragù was added
after the Spanish introduced
the tomato into Italy
in the 16th century.

SICILY, ITALY

ARANCINO

MAKES UP TO 15 ARANCINI

A deep-fried fistful of flavour, the *arancino* (or *arancina* if you're from Palermo) – a golden croquette of rice, meat and cheese – is the king of Sicilian street food.

METHOD

1 Cook the rice in lightly salted boiling water.

2 Mix the saffron powder with the egg yolks, and add to the drained rice.

3 Stir in the grated pecorino (or parmesan) cheese and butter.

4 Spread the rice mix out on a large plate to cool for up to two hours.

5 Fry the onion in butter and a couple of tablespoons of olive oil until softened.

6 Add the mince, and cook for a few minutes. Add the red wine.

7 Dilute the tomato paste in a glass of water; add to the mince when the wine has virtually evaporated.

8 Add salt and pepper to taste and cook on a moderate heat for about 20 minutes.

9 While the ragù is simmering, cook the peas in water and a tablespoon of olive oil for about 10 minutes, then add them to the mince.

10 Take enough rice mix to form a flattened patty on your hand. Make an indentation in the middle and fill it with a spoonful of ragù and two or three cubes of cheese. Place a second patty of rice mix on top of the first and shape into a ball.

11 Coat the ball with egg and breadcrumbs.

12 Fry the ball in oil heated to about 180°C (350°F). When it's a rich orange-gold colour, remove, and drain of oil. Repeat for each ball.

13 Serve hot or at room temperature.

TASTING NOTES

Although they're a Sicilian icon, *arancini* combine flavours from the whole of Italy: risotto from Milan, ragù from Bologna and cheese from southern Italy. For the best experience, join the locals in a Sicilian cafe and eat yours standing at the bar. Here they'll be piled up like cannonballs and handed out by well-drilled bar staff. Eating one is a messy operation. Once you've bitten through the crunchy coating, you'll have to contend with fallout from seeping rice, escaping peas, and strings of melted cheese. But don't worry. This is Sicily, where even simple bar snacks are enjoyed with operatic gusto. ● *by Duncan Garwood*

AREPAS REINA PEPIADA

YOU'LL NEED
2½ cups lukewarm water
2 tsp salt
2 cups cornflour (preferably Venezuelan Harina PAN)
2 tsp oil (try coconut oil), plus more for the griddle/pan

For the filling
2 large chicken breasts, poached and finely shredded
1 large avocado, lightly mashed
½ cup mayonnaise or Greek yoghurt
¼ cup chopped coriander
½ lime, juiced
salt and pepper, for seasoning

ORIGINS

Purportedly adapted from a staple food of pre-Hispanic Amerindian tribes that lived in the northern Andes of Venezuela, arepas got their name from the indigenous name for corn bread, 'erepa'. Spanish colonisation saw this simple dish diffused throughout Gran Colombia (now Venezuela, Colombia, Ecuador and Panama) and to this day, arepas stuffed with fillings (known as *arepas rellena*) remain the region's most prevalent street food snack.

JUPITERIMAGES © GETTY IMAGES, KRZYSZTOF DYDYNSKI © GETTY IMAGES, JUANMONINO © GETTY IMAGES

MAKES 8

VENEZUELA

AREPAS

Like tacos to Mexico and burgers to the US, these cornbread 'sandwiches' are part of Venezuela's national identity – and the ultimate vehicle for an array of savoury fillings.

METHOD

1 In a bowl, combine the shredded chicken, avocado, mayonnaise or yoghurt, coriander and lime juice, and season to taste before refrigerating while you make the arepas.

2 In a bowl, stir together the water and salt. Gradually add the cornmeal, mixing the ingredients together with your hands, using your fingers to dissolve any lumps.

3 Add the oil and continue mixing with your hands until completely smooth, and soft enough that the mixture does not crack when moulded.

4 Divide the dough into 8 equal parts, roll into balls, then flatten into discs approximately 2.5cm (1in) thick, and 12cm (4.5in) in diameter.

5 Place the discs on a pre-heated, greased griddle or large sauté pan, and cook for about 5 minutes until the side you're cooking has golden-brown splotches.

6 Turn over and cook for an additional 5 minutes before removing from the griddle. With a sharp knife, split open the arepas but don't cut them in half entirely.

7 Spoon the chicken mixture into the pockets and serve.

TASTING NOTES

Sturdy and compact with a crisp outer edge and soft, dense interior, Venezuela's carbohydrate of choice makes the perfect (if messy) meal on the run. The best *arepas* are griddled to perfection right in front of you before being filled with anything from mild cheese to smoky pulled pork. With each different stuffing, the name of the *arepa* playfully changes. Served plain, it's known as a *viuda* – a widow. With black beans and white cheese it's a *dominó* (as in the gaming tiles) and with pork, a *rumbera* (rumba dancer). Arguably the most popular, however, is the *reina pepiada* (curvaceous queen). Stuffed with a zesty chicken and avocado salad, this version was named for Susana Duijm, a Venezuelan beauty queen crowned Miss World in 1955. ● *by Sarah Reid*

ORIGINS

Technically meatballs, *bakso* are almost always associated with their eponymous soup that's sold by street vendors around Indonesia. The name originates from the Hokkien word for shredded meat so the dish is likely of Chinese-Indonesian origin. Today *bakso* has travelled all over Southeast Asia to be mixed into myriad tasty broths from Vietnam to Singapore. No matter what regional ingredients are added, the dish always keeps the three basics: meatballs, noodles and broth.

YOU'LL NEED

For the meatballs
3 tbs diced shallot
1lb ground beef or chicken
3 tbs tapioca starch
1 egg white
1 tbs sugar
vegetable oil, for frying
salt and pepper, for seasoning

For the broth
3 cloves garlic, crushed
1 tbs ginger, grated
1.8l (60fl oz) beef or
   chicken stock
1 stalk celery, whole
1 tsp sugar
1 tsp pepper
1 tsp lime juice
1 tsp fish sauce
vegetable oil
salt to taste
400g (14oz) egg or rice
   noodles, cooked al dente

Optional garnishes
1 bunch bok choi, blanched
spring onion, chopped
fried shallots
boiled eggs, chopped
sambal (chilli sauce), to taste

SERVES 6

JAVA, INDONESIA

BAKSO

Subtly seasoned broth and tasty meatballs are the culinary equivalent of a warm hug. Take a break from regional, fiery spices to enjoy Indonesia's most humble, yet well-loved street food.

METHOD

For the meatballs

1 Fry the shallots in the vegetable oil in a small pan over medium heat until golden.

2 Transfer to a food processor and add the meat, tapioca starch, egg white, sugar and seasoning and process until very well ground. Place the paste in a bowl and refrigerate, covered, for at least two hours.

3 Put a pot of water on to boil. While waiting, form the meat paste into balls about an inch in diameter.

4 Drop the meatballs into the boiling water. Once each ball floats to the surface of the water, cook them an additional two minutes. Set aside.

For the broth

1 Lightly sauté the garlic and ginger in a small frying pan until fragrant.

2 Add to a large pot with the stock and celery and simmer for several minutes.

3 Remove the celery stalk and add remaining ingredients to taste.

4 Ladle into individual bowls and add meatballs to each. Garnish as desired.

TASTING NOTES

Portable *bakso* stalls, with their aluminium pot for broth and a shelf or two for meatballs, noodles, vegetables and other fixings, are often pedalled around by bicycle late afternoons through the night in Indonesia, from the smallest country town to exhaust-filled Jakarta. With its savoury, not-spicy broth, slippery noodles and gently seasoned meatballs, *bakso* is perfect sustenance for a stop on a long, curvy bus ride, a late night on the town or nourishment after a bout of tummy trouble. ● *by Celeste Brash*

ORIGINS

A seaside equivalent of the ubiquitous Turkish kebab, *balık ekmek* evolved when entrepreneurial fishermen in Istanbul decided to cut out the middle man and sell their wares direct to the hungry masses. Setting up grills right on their boats near the Galata Bridge, they fried fish while rolling with the swell of the Bosphorus, and served it up to appreciative porters, merchant sailors, commuters and stevedores who waited on the quayside.

SERVES 1

TURKEY

BALIK EKMEK

A fish sandwich to fill your fist (and stomach), *balık ekmek*
combines the best of Turkey: fresh fish, sweet tomatoes, olive oil,
zesty lemons, and camaraderie between cook and consumer.

YOU'LL NEED

Turkish pide bread
mackerel (or similar oily fish),
  filleted
olive oil
lettuce, roughly chopped
parsley, roughly chopped
white onion, roughly chopped
tomato, sliced
lemon, quartered
sumac
chilli powder
sweet paprika
salt

METHOD

1 Slice the pide bread lengthwise to 'butterfly' it.

2 Fry the mackerel fillets on a hot grill with a good splash of olive oil for three or four minutes each side.

3 When the fish is almost ready, rub the opened-out pide on the grill to absorb some oil and fishy flavour.

4 Place the fried fish in the pide, add a handful of lettuce, parsley and onion, and a few slices of tomato.

5 Squeeze lemon over the fish and salad.

6 Sprinkle with sumac, chilli powder, paprika and salt to taste.

TASTING NOTES

Start slowly – the fish is piping hot, and quite oily – and take care not to get a mouthful of the butcher's paper in which the sandwich is wrapped. Tuck into the light, spongy, white bread, which beautifully soaks up hot pan juices, lemon juice and fish oils. Once you get a taste of sweet mackerel offset with the tartness of citrus, you'll want to wolf it down. Crisp lettuce and onions lend the experience crunch and freshness, and the ruby tomatoes of a Turkish summer give it a sweetness that rounds out the salty smokiness of it all. It's beyond finger-lickin', it's wipe-your-chin-with-the-back-of-your-hand good! ● *by Will Gourlay*

YOU'LL NEED
8-10 dried shiitake
  mushrooms
½ tbs dried shrimp
230g (½lb) minced pork
a little cooking oil
3 tbs thick soy sauce
2-3 shallots, chopped
4 cups sticky rice, washed
  and drained
boiling water
optional garnishes: sweet
  chilli sauce, coriander leaves
  (cilantro)

ORIGINS

Zhutong fan (bamboo rice) owes
its existence to the nutritional
needs of indigenous tribal
hunter-gatherers, who roamed
the mountains and jungles of
the region and foraged, hunted
and cooked as and when they
could. It is thought that they
discovered this ingenious
method of carrying a sustaining
and nutritionally sound meal of
glutinous rice, boar meat and
locally harvested vegetables
inside a convenient, disposable
and easily stowed (in belt, quiver
or loincloth) bamboo stalk, and
the tradition has lived on.

TAIWAN

BAMBOO RICE

Is 'Think globally, act locally' your motto? You can't get any more local than this hearty steamed snack of bamboo stuffed with regionally sourced rice, vegetables and wild boar.

METHOD

1 Reconstitute the dried mushrooms and shrimp in hot water for 10 minutes and then chop into pieces.

2 Stir-fry the pork with the cooking oil in a hot wok until brown. Drain any excess oil.

3 Stir in the mushrooms, shrimp, soy sauce and shallots.

4 Divide the pork mixture between the bamboo cups or greased pudding bowls and press down firmly with a spoon.

5 Add rice, again packing down with a spoon, until each cup is about two-thirds full.

6 Add boiling water to just cover the rice in each cup.

7 Place the cups in a bamboo steamer. Alternatively you can place the cups directly in a large pot with about 5cm (2in) of water in the bottom, and cover with a lid.

8 Steam at a high heat for 30–35 minutes. Leave in the steamer for an additional 10 minutes with the heat off before serving.

9 To serve, you can either turn the rice out onto a plate, or leave it in the cups. It's great on its own or topped with a little sweet chilli sauce and coriander leaves.

TASTING NOTES

A 30-minute bus ride from Taipei brings you to the riverside mountain town of Wulai. In addition to boasting some of northern Taiwan's finest hiking and hot springs, it's here where you'll find *zhutong fan* (bamboo rice) stalls springing up in the winter months, when the bamboo is mature. Crack open a *zhutong fan* and peel off the outer layer like a banana skin. Then enjoy the sticky, savoury rice with its delicate fragrance of bamboo.

As this kind of bamboo can be hard to come by, we've provided an alternative method that can be much more easily followed at home. Using cups made from bamboo stalks will impart the flavour of the bamboo to the rice, but if you can't find these, use eight small pudding basins or rice bowls instead, greased with a little oil. ● *by Joshua Samuel Brown*

YOU'LL NEED

1 long crusty bread stick, halved then sliced lengthways
whole-egg mayonnaise
1 tin liver spread or coarse liver pâté
4 slices cooked pork belly, thinly sliced
4 slices *cha lua* (Vietnamese-style ham) or mortadella
4 slices cucumber
Maggi Seasoning or light soy sauce, to taste
2 red chillies, chopped
a handful of coriander leaves (cilantro)

For the pickle

1 tsp salt
125g (4½ oz) sugar
1 medium carrot, julienned
1 daikon, julienned
1 cup white wine vinegar
1 cup water

ORIGINS

Banh mi is an early example of fusion food. The dish's primary ingredients – baguette, mayonnaise and a type of pork-liver pâté – show an obvious link with the French, who introduced these foods to the Vietnamese under their tenure as colonial rulers during the early 20th century. Other ingredients, including *xa xiu*, the barbecued pork better known as *char siu*, have Chinese origins, while the herbs and seasonings are distinctively Southeast Asian.

TASTING NOTES

Banh mi is the epitome of street food; the sandwiches are sold almost exclusively from informal stalls and vendors across Vietnam. If there's any seating at all, it usually takes the form of tiny plastic stools, and the sandwiches are generally served to go, wrapped in recycled paper. Pâté? Meatballs or grilled pork? Chilli? Mayonnaise? Diners are asked to choose their meats, as well as their toppings and condiments. If you're feeling indecisive, you can go for *banh mi dac biet* ('special' *banh mi* that runs the gamut of Vietnamese-style charcuterie, from head cheese to steamed sausage). Regardless, the result is crispy, meaty, rich and spicy – the best of Southeast Asian cuisine in a Western package. ● *by Austin Bush*

VIETNAM

BANH MI

MAKES 2 SANDWICHES

Popular around the world, this toasted baguette stuffed with mayonnaise, pâté, meat, pickled vegetables and fresh herbs is a serious contender for the coveted title of world's best sandwich.

METHOD

1 Make the pickle at least an hour before using by sprinkling the salt and 2 tsp of the sugar on the carrot and daikon in a bowl.

2 Extract as much liquid as possible by pressing on the vegetables gently.

3 Rinse with cold water and press again to extract as much water as possible.

4 In a small saucepan, place the remaining sugar, vinegar and water on a low heat and stir the mixture together, until the sugar dissolves.

5 Pour the vinegar mixture over the vegetables and set aside for at least an hour.

6 To assemble the *banh mi*, spread some mayonnaise on the top half of the bread stick, and the liver spread on the bottom half.

7 Layer two slices each of the pork belly, ham and cucumber. Season with Maggi Seasoning or light soy sauce.

8 Drain the julienned carrot and daikon from the vinegar mixture and add to the sandwich.

9 Add the chillies and coriander. Serve.

REBECCA SKINNER © GETTY IMAGES

For the filling
250g (1½lb) minced pork
  (medium-lean)
3 scallions (spring onions),
  chopped
3 shiitake mushrooms,
  chopped
2 tbs ginger, finely chopped
2–3 garlic cloves, finely
  chopped
2 tbs dark soy sauce
1 tbs oyster sauce
1 tbs rice wine or sherry
1 tsp sugar
½ tsp sesame oil

For the dough
3 tbs melted lard
¾ cup hot water
400g (14oz) plain (all-purpose)
  flour
1½ tsp baking powder
2 tsp instant dry yeast
4 tbs sugar
1 tsp salt
¼ cup cold water

For baking
1 tbs sesame oil
baking parchment cut into 16
  squares of 7.5cm (3in) each

ORIGINS

Legend has it that this now-ubiquitous Chinese steamed bun was created by Zhuge Liang, the great military strategist and inventor of the Three Kingdoms period (AD220–280). While in the deep south of China his soldiers were struck down by the plague. Zhuge Liang made the buns to look like human heads and used them as both sustenance for the living and a sacrifice to the gods, and thus cured his troops' sickness. Mighty buns indeed.

CHINA

MAKES 8–10 LARGE BUNS

This billowy steamed, baked or fried bun, filled with anything from slow-cooked meat and fragrant pork broth to garish custard and sweet lotus-seed paste, is a popular morning snack.

METHOD

1 Mix together all the filling ingredients. Set aside for one hour minimum.

2 For the dough, mix the lard with half of the hot water. Then mix together all dry ingredients for the dough.

3 Pour 90 per cent of the dry mixture into the wet mixture, stirring vigorously with a tablespoon. Continue adding hot water until a dough begins to form, then add cold water. Knead for 7–8 minutes into a smooth, stiff dough. Add water as needed if it is too stiff to shape.

4 Allow the dough to sit and ferment until it has doubled in volume (at least 30 minutes). Then knead for a few minutes to de-gas.

5 Cut the dough into 16 sections. Roll each into a small ball, then flatten and shape into a thin disc approximately 11cm (4.5in) in diameter. Aim to keep the dough thin around the edges.

6 Spoon roughly 1 tbs of filling into each disc's centre. Crimp the edges together around the filling.

7 Brush sesame oil onto a square of baking parchment, then set the crimped bun onto it.

8 Allow the bun to rise again on a covered plate or tray for a further 20 minutes before placing in a steamer to cook for 15 minutes.

9 Serve the *baozi* hot.

TASTING NOTES

All over China, from dawn until after lunch (never, traditionally, at night), innumerable pots at roadside and dim sum outlets bubble and spit, steaming a million of these bite-sized buns in small bamboo baskets. Dipped in ginger vinegar or a splash of soy sauce, they're stodge of the finest kind. Freshness is everything, though, as they tend to sag as they cool, so try to eat them within a minute or two. You won't find it hard to scoff them down, but do beware: the broth is often volcanically hot. Make a small nick in the side and carefully suck out the juice, before wolfing down the rest in a greedy gulp. ● *by Tom Parker Bowles*

ORIGINS

The first written recipe for *bhelpuri* is attributed to an English army cook called William Harold, who was dispatched to the streets of colonial Bombay to bring back a list of ingredients for this delicious snack so it could be added to the menu in the officers' mess. However, Indians trace the origins of this spicy *chaat* back to the Maratha leader Chhatrapati Shivaji Maharaj, who demanded a snack that could be prepared and consumed on the way to battle.

YOU'LL NEED

For the tamarind chutney

¼ cup fresh or dried tamarind
½ cup deseeded dates
½ cup jaggery (or soft brown sugar)
½ tsp ground cumin seed
¼ tsp ground dried chilli
¼ tsp salt

For the mint chutney

1 cup coriander leaves (cilantro)
½ cup mint leaves
3 green chillies, deseeded
1 tbs lime juice
salt, to taste
water

For the bhelpuri

½ cup boiled potato, finely chopped
½ cup tomato, finely chopped
½ cup red onion, finely chopped
3 green chillies, deseeded and chopped
¼ cup coriander leaves (cilantro), finely chopped
¼ cup tamarind chutney
¼ cup mint chutney
1 tbs grated ginger
1 tbs garam masala powder
salt, to taste
¾ cup *sev*
1 cup puffed rice
1 lemon, cut into quarters

SERVES 2

MUMBAI, INDIA

BHELPURI

A fiery constellation of vegetables, pulses, spices and chutney, *bhelpuri* is a perfect mirror for the melting-pot city that created it. It's salad, Jim, but not as you know it.

METHOD

For the tamarind chutney

1 Remove the seeds from your tamarind, and mash the flesh into a pulp with ½ cup of water.

2 Squeeze the mixture through a sieve to create ½ cup tamarind water; add to a pan with the remaining ingredients, bring to the boil, then simmer for about 10 minutes.

3 Allow the mixture to cool, then pass through a blender to create a smooth paste. Chill before serving.

For the mint chutney

Finely chop the coriander leaves, mint and chillies, then blend into a fine paste with the lime juice, salt and a little water.

For the bhelpuri

1 In a large bowl, mix together the vegetables, chillies, most of the coriander (reserve some for use as a garnish), chutneys and spices.

2 Add the *sev* and puffed rice to the mix, stir and serve immediately with a squeeze of lemon juice and a sprinkle of coriander leaves.

TASTING NOTES

Bhelpuri will put your taste buds through their paces. First comes the crunch, from the rice puffs and crispy *sev* noodles. Next comes the tang – thanks to the tamarind chutney. Then comes the chilli hit, riding on a wave of masala spices, followed by lingering sweet, salty and sour aftertastes. Many sit-down restaurants serve their own interpretations, but the best *bhelpuri* comes from street stalls and hawker stands, served on paper plates and prepared on the spot to keep all the ingredients firm and fragrant. Traditionally, *bhelpuri* is scooped from plate to mouth with the fingers of the right hand, but most vendors will provide a plastic spoon or fork if you ask. ● *by Joe Bindloss*

MAKES 4 BURRITOS

YOU'LL NEED

8 strips bacon
2 potatoes, grated
1–2 tbs vegetable oil
1 tsp butter
8 eggs, lightly beaten
½ cup (or more) New Mexico
  green chillies, roasted,
  peeled and chopped
4 flour tortillas
salt and pepper, to taste

ORIGINS

Tia Sophia's, a classic diner in Santa Fe, claims to have invented the breakfast burrito in the 1970s. But its version is a plated dish, smothered in red or green chilli sauce – delicious, but hardly portable. It's not clear who first made the smaller, tidier handheld version, before Taco Bell and McDonald's started serving it nationwide in the 1980s. But New Mexicans know these versions are imposters, as they lack the essential chunks of green chilli.

NEW MEXICO, USA

BREAKFAST BURRITO

This is a rancher's breakfast rendered portable by its flour-tortilla wrapper. Rolled up inside is scrambled eggs, home fries or hash-browns, bacon or sausage, and lashings of chilli.

METHOD

1 Cook the bacon to your preference; set aside to cool, then tear into 2.5cm (1in) pieces. Wipe any burned pieces out of the skillet (frying pan) and pour off surplus grease.

2 Make the hash browns. Set a heavy-bottomed skillet on a medium heat. Squeeze out any liquid from the potatoes, then toss with salt and pepper. Add 1 tbs oil to the skillet, then arrange the potatoes in an even layer. Fry on a medium heat until browned on the bottom, then flip and cook till crispy (you may need to flip repeatedly to avoid burning; you may also need additional oil). Set aside on a paper towel. Cut into 5cm (2in) pieces.

3 Prepare the eggs. Wipe the skillet clean, then heat the butter on medium-low heat until bubbling. Add a pinch of salt to the beaten egg and pour into the skillet. Stir slowly until cooked to your liking. Remove from the skillet and set aside.

4 Set up your assembly line: bacon, hash browns, scrambled eggs and green chilli. Have one large plate for working on, and four more for serving (or foil to wrap up the burritos).

5 Wipe the skillet clean and place over high heat. Heat a tortilla in the skillet until slightly puffed and dotted with brown spots, flipping it several times.

6 Place the tortilla on a plate and lay out a quarter of the scrambled eggs horizontally in the centre. Add a quarter of the hash browns, then chilli and bacon, spreading the ingredients evenly.

7 Roll up the burrito, starting with the bottom third folded up over the eggs, then each end folded over, then rolling the remainder tightly away from you.

TASTING NOTES

Wrapped in foil and warm to the touch, the breakfast burrito is an enigma. There's no way to gauge the quality until you bite in. But not too fast – you can't get greedy and unwrap more than an inch or so at a time, or you'll wind up with your breakfast in your lap. A quality specimen, ideally served in a dim, family-run corner store, on a back road to a great hiking trail, has crispy potatoes and a generous amount of green chilli and bacon, structured so that each bite contains a bit of everything. ● *by Zora O'Neill*

ORIGINS

The origins of the Tunisian *brik* can be traced to the Turkish *börek* (from which its name is also derived), an ancient invention that migrated to Anatolia with the people from central Asian Turkistan hundreds of years ago. Today, according to Tunisian tradition, if a young man spills any yolk of a special *brik* prepared by his prospective wife's mother, he may not be allowed to wed. The *brik* is customarily the food used to break the Ramadan fast.

YOU'LL NEED

170g (6oz) tinned tuna
2 tbs parsley, chopped
2 tbs grated parmesan
salt
pepper
1 small onion, finely chopped (optional)
4 outer shells (*malsouka* or substitute egg/spring roll wrappers)
4 eggs
olive oil, for deep-frying
lemon
harissa (optional)

TUNISIA

BRIK

MAKES 4

A deep-fried pastry packet filled with egg, tuna, onion, harissa and parsley, the *brik* is a study of compatible contrasts: crispy and soft, fresh and salty, mild and tangy.

METHOD

1 Combine the tuna, parsley and parmesan with salt and pepper to taste. Add lightly sauteed onion if desired. Divide this mixture into four equal parts.

2 Add one portion of the mixture to the centre of each of four outer shells. Break an egg over the top of each one, making sure it stays in place (it helps to make a small well in the mixture to hold the egg).

3 Fold the wrappers (which should be square) in half along the diagonal to make a triangular shape. Slide them into a pan of hot olive oil (about 1cm (½in) deep). Fry for a couple of minutes until golden brown on one side and then flip. Do the same to the other side.

4 Set aside the *briks* to drain. Then sprinkle with lemon juice and serve hot.

TIP *Have harissa on hand for extra spice when serving. Alternatively, the harissa may be added to the mixture before it is cooked.*

TASTING NOTES

The most common, inexpensive and delicious street treat in Tunisia, the *brik* is practically a daily necessity for any traveller on a budget, anyone who likes to chat with locals, and, frankly, anyone with taste buds. Part of the delight of the experience of a *brik* is lining up with everyone else at a street cart or hole-in-the-wall market stall in the middle of a buzzing souk, admiring the slick movements of the *brik*-maker and then savouring the airy and soft, crisp and crusty textures and fresh Mediterranean flavours. Watch how deftly practised *brik*-eaters keep the soft yolk from spilling! ● *by Ethan Gelber*

ORIGINS

Moroccans don't give much credence to the saying that breakfast is the most important meal of the day: a glass of sweet tea and a piece of bread often suffices. But workers need something more substantial, and *bsarra* is a dish to fill the hole. Soup shops open early to cater to demand, and are washing up their pots by lunchtime – *bsarra* tends to run out by the time that the call to midday prayers rings through the medina.

SERVES 2-4

FEZ, MOROCCO

BSARRA

Served with a hunk of bread, *bsarra* is a thick soup of broad beans that is cooked in cauldrons on the streets of Morocco – the perfect breakfast-on-the-go.

YOU'LL NEED

500g (1lb) dried skinless broad beans (fava beans)
4 cups water
8 garlic cloves, crushed
1 tsp salt
olive oil
cumin
paprika

METHOD

1 Soak the broad beans in water overnight, then drain and rinse.

2 Bring the water to the boil and add the beans, crushed garlic and salt. Simmer for at least 30 minutes, until the beans are well cooked.

3 Blend in a food processor.

4 Serve with a generous drizzle of olive oil and a sprinkle of cumin and paprika.

TASTING NOTES

Bsarra shops tend to be hole-in-the-wall places: open-fronted with a soup vat in the front, and enough space behind for half a dozen people to squeeze around a bench. Rough bowls and battered spoons are the order of the day. The lake of olive oil that accompanies the soup might look excessive, but it deepens the taste and gives a smooth texture. Be generous with the cumin and paprika, and add salt to taste. Some people dip their bread, while others tear it into the soup. Either way, save a crust to clean the bowl with at the end. Wash *bsarra* down with mint tea and you're set for a day exploring the souks. ● *by Paul Clammer*

ORIGINS

In the middle of Hanoi's rapidly modernising cityscape, the preparation of *bún cha* is continuing as it has done for centuries. A single multitasking vendor often does it all, hunched over a charcoal grill, methodically fanning the embers to obtain the optimum amount of heat. Fuelled by unctuous fat dripping onto hot coals, lots of billowing smoke is essential to maximise the pork's fragrant marinade, and plates of fresh herbs are traditionally sourced from the nearby village of Lang.

YOU'LL NEED

500g (1lb) pork belly, sliced thinly
4 tbs fish sauce
2 tbs spring onions, chopped
2 tbs Chinese chives, chopped
4 tsp soy sauce
4 red Asian shallots, chopped
4 cloves garlic, crushed
500g (1lb) thin rice noodles, prepared as per packet directions
200g (7oz) beanshoots, trimmed
1 head of lettuce, shredded
large handful fresh Thai basil leaves
large handful fresh Vietnamese mint leaves
large handful fresh coriander leaves (cilantro)

For the dressing

2 tbs fish sauce
2 tbs white wine vinegar
2 tbs sugar
½ cup water
1 red chilli, chopped
2 garlic cloves, crushed
1 tbs lime juice

SERVES 4

HANOI, VIETNAM

BÚN CHA

Bún cha's fragrant combo of grilled pork, fresh herbs and vermicelli noodles is now found across Vietnam, but the best flavours are still in the street food kitchens of Hanoi.

METHOD

1 Combine the fish sauce, spring onions, chives, soy sauce, shallots and garlic in a shallow bowl.

2 Add the pork and marinate in the fridge for at least two hours or preferably overnight.

3 Combine all the dressing ingredients and bring them to a boil in a saucepan over medium heat. Set aside.

4 Grill the pork over medium-high heat for a few minutes on each side.

5 Assemble the salad on individual plates with a handful each of noodles, beanshoots, lettuce, herbs and pork. Pour over some dressing and serve.

TIP *A handful of shiso leaves (also known as perilla leaves), if you can find them, will add extra oomph to this delightfully herby dish.*

TASTING NOTES

To find *bún cha*, sharpen your sense of smell and look for the mini-clouds of fragrant smoke drifting through the labyrinth of Hanoi's Old Quarter. The most humble of *bún cha* places is just a charcoal grill and a few kid-size pieces of furniture. Pull up a chair and bite into the smoky and caramelised pork, grilled on the outside, but moist and delicate to the taste. *Bún cha* is also the ultimate DIY meal; just stir in more sweetly fragrant broth, slivers of green pawpaw, or fresh herbs, chilli and garlic for a customised combination of pork and vermicelli noodles. A side order of crunchy *nem cua be* (crab spring rolls) is recommended for the ultimate Hanoi lunch. ● *by Brett Atkinson*

ORIGINS

Immigrant Indian plantation workers in Durban were often banned from cafes during South Africa's apartheid era, so the community created bunny chow in the late 1940s as a way for the workers to carry their meals into the fields with them (necessity is the mother of invention).

It's believed that the name originates from the city's banyan trees, under which the vendors used to sit to sell their portable bread-loaf curries in the shade.

YOU'LL NEED

½ cup oil
1 onion, chopped
1 star anise
1 cinnamon stick
3 whole cardamom pods
½ tsp fennel seeds
½ tsp cumin seed
3 tbs garam masala
2 tsp turmeric
1 tsp ground coriander
1 tsp cayenne pepper
2 medium tomatoes, chopped
1kg (2lb) lamb or beef, cut into 2.5cm (1in) cubes
6 curry leaves
2 teaspoons ground ginger
4 garlic cloves, finely chopped
2 large potatoes, cut into 2.5cm (1in) cubes
1 small loaf white bread (unsliced)

SERVES 2

DURBAN, KWAZULU-NATAL, SOUTH AFRICA

BUNNY CHOW

Cute name. Powerful story. One heck of a meal. Put simply, it's a rich Indian curry served in a hollowed out loaf of bread.

METHOD

1 Heat the oil in a pan before frying up the onion with the star anise, cinnamon, cardamom pods, fennel seeds and cumin seeds.

2 When the onion is soft and glassy, stir in the garam masala, turmeric, ground coriander and cayenne pepper. After a few minutes add the tomatoes, continuing to stir.

3 Add the meat, curry leaves, ground ginger and garlic. Simmer for at least 30 minutes, adding a little water if it gets too dry.

4 When the meat is almost tender, add the potatoes. Continue to simmer until the potatoes are cooked through.

5 Meanwhile, put the bread loaf on its side and cut it in half. Using a sharp knife, remove most of the soft white bread centres from each section, being careful to leave thick walls and a bottom on each.

6 Ladle the finished curry into the bread bowls, and place the section of bread you removed atop the filled hollow.

TASTING NOTES

Eating bunny chow, or 'bunnies' as they are affectionately known, is as much about the experience as the meal itself. Utensils are not used – it is a hands-on affair. The piece of bread that comes atop your serving, which was removed to make way for the steaming curry of your choice, is your best tool to help you extricate the savoury dish. And as you work your way down the bread bowl, its saturated self is also up for grabs. Whether you've bought your bunny chow streetside or made it at home, spare a moment to remember what necessitated its creation. ● *by Matt Phillips*

ORIGINS

Found in different forms across the Balkans and beyond, *burek* originates in Turkey (where it is known as *börek*). The name comes from the Turkish *burmak* ('to twist'). As the Turkish Ottoman Empire expanded from the 14th to the 18th centuries, this tasty pastry moved with it, assuming different ingredients, forms and additives. In Bosnia, *burek* can be eaten at any hour: for breakfast accompanied by black tea, or after a busy night in the bars of Sarajevo's Baščaršija district.

TASTING NOTES

Though *burek* can be eaten either hot or cold, it's best straight from the oven. The pastry will be nicely flaky on the outside – yielding a pleasing 'crunch' as you bite into it – but on the inside, where it is moistened by the contents, it should be tender, with the consistency of perfectly cooked pasta. The contents should be moist, but not gooey, offsetting the crisp outer layers. Brushed with butter or olive oil, the whole affair is slightly greasy. In Bosnia it is cooked in great spirals in round baking trays. Choose which variety you want, and the baker will slice it with a pizza cutter and wrap it in butcher's paper for you. ● *by Will Gourlay*

SERVES 4

BOSNIA & HERCEGOVINA

BUREK

Crisp yet moist, hearty yet subtly spiced, *burek* is *the* Balkan street food. It's savoury and filling and will fuel you through a day exploring mountain villages or market towns.

YOU'LL NEED

3 onions, diced
750g (1½lb) minced (ground) beef or lamb
1 tbs sweet paprika
1 tbs allspice
½ tsp cinnamon
4 sheets filo pastry
¼ cup melted butter (or olive oil)
1 beaten egg (optional)

METHOD

1 Heat the oven to around 200°C (400°F).

2 Fry the onions until soft and almost caramelised.

3 Add the mince and fry until browned and slightly crumbly (drain off excess moisture or fat).

4 Remove the pan from the heat, add the paprika, allspice and cinnamon, stir through and allow the meat mixture to cool.

5 Place a single sheet of filo pastry on a bench, and brush lightly with melted butter (or olive oil).

6 Spread a quarter of the meat mixture along one edge of the filo pastry.

7 Roll the pastry sheet up to form a long tube enclosing the meat mixture, then twist the tube into a 'snail shell' spiral. Repeat three more times with the remaining ingredients.

8 Brush with more butter or oil (or egg if desired) and place in oven.

9 Bake for 20–30 minutes or until golden. Alternatively, use a filling of crumbled feta cheese, parsley and dill, or spinach sauteed with diced onion and dill.

YOU'LL NEED

250g (½lb) each of minced
  beef and pork (substitute
  lamb for pork, if desired)
diced garlic (amount to taste)
1 egg, beaten
½ tsp bicarb soda (baking
  soda)
¼ cup of hot (not boiling)
  water
½ tbs sweet paprika
pinch cayenne pepper or
  ground red
  chilli (optional)
pita or other flatbread
white onion, diced
ajvar (optional)
sour cream or yoghurt
  (optional)

ORIGINS

Ćevapčiči arrived in the Balkans
with the Ottoman Turks in the
15th century and gradually
spread through southeastern
Europe. It was part of a hearty
and simple meal – minced meat,
bread and onions – that could
sustain farmers, soldiers and
wanderers through the day.

CROATIA

ĆEVAPČIĆI

Laced with garlic and coupled with raw onions, ćevapčići are spicy skinless sausages that will fill your tummy and keep vampires away (and probably romantic prospects as well).

METHOD

1 Place all the ingredients except the bread, onion and optional accompaniments into a large mixing bowl.

2 Using your hands, mix all the ingredients together, ensuring that beef and pork mince blend thoroughly and that the garlic and paprika are distributed evenly.

3 Refrigerate for two hours (or longer) to allow the garlic and paprika to infuse the mixture.

4 Remove the bowl from fridge, then take a handful of mixture and fashion it into a short 'sausage' that will fit into your palm. Repeat until all mixture is used.

5 Cook the ćevapčići on a grill preheated to medium hot, turning once and allowing about 3–4 minutes each side, or until they are a rich golden brown.

6 Serve with flatbread and diced onion, and with *ajvar*, sour cream or yoghurt if desired.

TASTING NOTES

Ćevapčići are more than just an eating experience: there's the sound – the sizzle of the hotplate – and the scent – the aroma of charcoal embers and the tang of frying meat. You won't need a knife to get started, just a fork – or your hand if you're wrapping each individual ćevapčić in flat somun or pita bread. The piquancy of the garlic will be released with the first bite, and you'll experience a gentle snap at each mouthful: the meat is firm but tender, chewy but not gristly. Dip each ćevapčić into ajvar or yoghurt to experience the melding of flavours; intersperse this with forkfuls of diced onion. ● *by Will Gourlay*

YOU'LL NEED

1 red onion, thinly sliced
500–675g (1–11/2lb) sea bass
   fillets, skinned and chopped
   into large, bitesized pieces
pinch of red chilli flakes
1 clove garlic, peeled and
   grated
juice of 5 limes
500g (1lb) sweet potatoes
1 corn on the cob, chopped
   into 5cm (2in) pieces
5 tbs olive oil
3 tsp rice vinegar
¼ tsp caster sugar
½ *aji limo* (use normal red
   chilli pepper if unavailable),
   seeded and chopped
grated rind of 1 lime
2 small avocados, peeled,
   stoned and sliced
3 tbs chopped coriander
   leaves (cilantro)
salt
ground black pepper

ORIGINS

The Inca marinated fish to
cook them, but used *chicha*,
a fermented corn drink,
rather than the citrus that
features these days. Spanish
conquistadors brought the limes
that became bona fide ceviche
marinade. Corvina, prevalent
on Peru's coast, became
traditionally used. Japanese-
Peruvian chef Dario Matsufuji
shook up a century-old recipe
and reduced marinating time
from hours to minutes in the
1970s, which became the
preparation method to emulate.

PACIFIC COAST, PERU

CEVICHE DE CORVINA

SERVES 6 AS A STARTER

Combining the marinated fish and chilli peppers the Inca would have known, zesty Spanish-introduced citrus and a makeover from a Peruvian-Japanese chef, Peru's national dish is the ultimate fusion cuisine.

METHOD

1 Lay half the red onion slices in a large glass bowl with the fish on top. Sprinkle over the chilli flakes and grated garlic, then cover with lime juice.

2 Cover the bowl and chill. Professional ceviche-makers in Peru now use the quick marinade which, when preparing large quantities, helps keep the fish fresh, but this is an acquired art and a two-hour marinade is recommended for home cooks. During the chilling/marinating process, spoon the lime juice over the fish again once or twice.

3 Meanwhile, boil the sweet potatoes and corn for 30 minutes. Drain and place to one side.

4 Whisk together the oil, rice vinegar and caster sugar until smooth. Then whisk in the chopped ají limo/chilli pepper and grated lime rind.

5 When the fish is done, drain and discard the lime juice.

6 Add the fish to the oil/rice vinegar/caster sugar and mix well. Add the diced sweet potato and avocado and mix again.

7 Add the final half of the red onion along with the coriander leaves and the corn on the cob pieces and season to taste. Serve immediately.

TASTING NOTES

The sharp kick of the lime, the crunch of red onions and the fiery red-yellow of Peruvian chilli pepper *ají limo* mingle with the taste of soft white corvina (a Pacific sea bass) as it breaks into chunks in your mouth. Then your palate grasps the sweet potato and corn that counterbalance the feisty fish with an earthiness that reminds you what a unique thing ceviche de corvina is in a country where most street snacks are carbohydrate-dominated. Unlike many street foods, presentation is also key. The onion-and-chilli-pepper garnish sits on top of the fish, encircled by the sweet potato, corn clumps and hunks of avocado. Proper ceviche is an assault on the eyes as well as the taste buds. ● *by Luke Waterson*

YOU'LL NEED

500g boneless chicken, cut
  into chunks
1 tsp ginger, grated
1 tsp garlic, crushed
10 curry leaves
5-6 whole green chillies
1 cup vegetable oil
1 tbs coriander, chopped

For the marinade
2 tsp of red Kashmiri chilli
  powder
1 tsp grated ginger
1 tsp crushed garlic
½ tsp turmeric powder
½ tsp ground black pepper
1 tbs lemon juice
Pinch of salt

For the sauce
1 cup natural yoghurt
1 tsp of red Kashmiri chilli
  powder
½ tsp of red food colouring
½ tsp turmeric powder
½ tsp coriander powder
Pinch of salt

For the batter
1 egg
2 tbs of cornflour
1 tbs of rice flour
1 tbs water

ORIGINS

When A. M. Buhari, the
proprietor of Chennai's Buhari
Hotel, invented Chicken 65 in
1965, he had no idea what he
was starting. The civic-minded
hotelier decided not to patent
the recipe for his phenomenally
popular chicken snack and
hawkers took it to the streets in
droves. Buhari didn't stop there
– Chicken 65 was followed by
Chicken 78 in 1978, Chicken 82
in 1982 and Chicken 90 in 1990.

SERVES 4

CHENNAI, INDIA

CHICKEN 65

Chennai's favourite non-veg snack is devil red, and devilishly spicy – the perfect accompaniment to a cold Kingfisher on a steamy South Indian afternoon.

METHOD

1 Mix all the marinade ingredients together in a stain-proof bowl and combine with the chicken until thoroughly coated. Allow to marinate for at least an hour.

2 Combine all the sauce ingredients in a bowl, and set aside.

3 For the batter, beat the egg and combine with the other batter ingredients until they form a smooth paste; stir together with the marinated chicken.

4 In a wok, heat a cup of vegetable oil and deep-fry the chicken on a medium flame till golden. Set aside on a piece of kitchen towel to absorb the excess oil.

5 Discard the frying oil and add 2 tbs of fresh vegetable oil to your pan. Saute the ginger and garlic for a few seconds until aromatic then add the curry leaves and green chillies and the battered chicken pieces.

6 Add the yoghurt mixture and cook on a medium flame until it is almost absorbed and the chicken pieces are almost dry.

7 Garnish your devil-red chicken pieces with chopped coriander and serve.

TASTING NOTES

You can still find the original Chicken 65 at the restaurant where it was invented, but the street-side offering is just as delicious. And even in its streetwise incarnation, this is one snack that looks great on a plate – candy apple-red chicken pieces tossed together with whole green chillies, curry leaves and chopped coriander. Perfect Chicken 65 should be served straight from the pan, still sizzling but moist and tender inside its chilli and spice jacket. The flavours should hit you in waves – chilli, garlic, ginger, pepper, coriander. It's lip-smackingly good and will leave a tingle on your lips that is best quenched with an ice-cold bottle of Kingfisher. ● *by Joe Bindloss*

ORIGINS

Singapore's most beloved dish is said to have first become a craze after a married street-chef couple began wok-cooking quartered mud crab in a mildly spicy chili sauce and selling the dish from their push cart. Success soon spawned imitators, and the chilli crab is now considered as Singaporean as Hainan Chicken Rice – much to the chagrin of some Malaysians, who consider the tasty seafood dish the intellectual property of their country.

YOU'LL NEED

1 kg (2.2lb) hard shell crab
2 onions, chopped
8 small red chillies, chopped
3 tsp vegetable oil
3 tsp shrimp paste
1 cup passata (tomato sauce)
¼ cup light soy sauce
¼ cup sugar
1 tbs tomato paste
2 tsp white vinegar
½ tsp salt
¼ tsp cornflour mixed in
    ½ cup of water
1 egg, lightly beaten

SERVES 2

SINGAPORE

CHILLI CRAB

Promoted as a national dish by the Singapore Tourism board, no visit to the Lion City would be complete without tasting sweet and spicy chilli crab.

METHOD

1 Chop the crab into quarters after removing the top shell. Cracking the claws at this stage not only allows for easier eating later, but will result in a more even flavour.

2 Blend the onion and chilli together to form a puree.

3 Heat the oil in a large wok on a medium-high heat. Fry up the onion and chili puree with the shrimp paste for about five minutes, or until the mixture changes colour.

4 Add the passata, soy sauce, sugar, tomato sauce, tomato paste, vinegar, salt and cornflour/water mix. Mix thoroughly and bring to the boil.

5 Add the crab pieces and cook, covered, over a medium heat for 8–10 minutes, turning occasionally, until the shells turn red and the crab is cooked through.

6 Toss the egg in mixture and stir for a minute to coat the crab chunks. Serve immediately.

TASTING NOTES

The texture of the meat found by peeling the shell from your order of chilli crab should be firm yet velvety. You'll know this before you've even popped a chunk in your mouth, as the dish is best eaten with one's hands. The tomato-based sauce that gives the dish half its name is a mixture of sweet and spicy, and a good plate of chilli crab shouldn't lean too far in either direction. To do so would take away from the flavour of the dish's main star, the crab itself, whose meat bursts with notes of savoury sweetness. ● *by Joshua Samuel Brown*

ORIGINS

The *chivito* dates back to circa 1950, when a woman stopped in at Antonio Carbonaro's restaurant in Punta del Este asking for *chivito* (grilled goat). Señor Carbonaro, finding himself goatless, improvised a sandwich of steak, ham and other goodies. The combination was so tasty that he added it to the menu, and within a couple of years was selling enough *chivitos* to keep two butchers in business. While none of the subsequent variations has involved goat, the name endures.

SERVES 1 (OR 2 LIGHTER EATERS!)

URUGUAY

CHIVITO AL PAN

This overloaded steak, ham and egg sandwich – Uruguay's flamboyant national speciality – offers one of the cheapest, tastiest and most accessible ways to sample the country's famous beef.

YOU'LL NEED

1 bap or bread roll, sliced in two lengthways
1 tbs mayonnaise
2 rashers of bacon
1 fillet steak
1 slice ham
1 slice mozzarella cheese
1 egg, boiled and thinly sliced
2 slices tomato
lettuce leaves

METHOD

1 Spread the mayonnaise on both slices of the bap or bread roll.

2 In a lightly oiled pan, fry the bacon rashers until crisp. Set aside the cooked bacon.

3 In the same pan, cook the fillet steak as preferred. Just after turning the steak, place the ham and cheese on top and cook until the steak is ready and the cheese melted.

4 To assemble the *chivito*, place the steak, ham and cheese on the bottom slice of bread and then add the bacon, egg, tomato and lettuce. Top with the other slice of bread and serve with plenty of napkins.

TIP *This recipe is for the basic, traditional* chivito *sandwich, but feel free to improvise and add as many extras as you can handle, such as pickles, olives, mushrooms, and pickled or grilled red peppers.*

TASTING NOTES

You'll find *chivitos* everywhere in Uruguay, from streetside stalls to restaurants. For the best experience, choose a spot where you can observe the chef, listen to the sizzle of grilling meat and watch as the cheese is melted on top, the bread toasted alongside, the tomato and lettuce tucked into place, and the crowning shake of salt added.

Stretch your fingers before you start – you'll need two hands and lots of napkins! A fully piled *chivito* can rise to ludicrous proportions. Most places slice it into two halves and valiantly attempt to hold it together with toothpicks; even so, eating it can be a challenge. Don't worry about the mess – a good *chivito* is meant to be juicy! ● *by Gregor Clark*

ORIGINS

Chole batura is from the Punjab, where it's a breakfast staple. It became a Delhi staple when migrants flooded into the city from what is now Pakistan after Partition in 1947. One of Delhi's best outlets was founded by the owner's grandfather, who arrived over 60 years ago with his recipe; he and his descendants have sold the dish from a shop in Paharganj ever since.

YOU'LL NEED

For the chole

1½ cups chickpeas (canned or soaked overnight)
2 tbs ghee or cooking oil
1 onion, finely chopped
1cm ginger, very finely chopped
2 cloves garlic, very finely chopped
1 tsp red chilli powder
pinch salt
1 tsp ground coriander seeds
¼ tsp turmeric powder
¼ tsp garam masala
2 tomatoes, blanched, peeled and chopped
1 tbs tamarind paste
half a glass of hot water

For the batura

2 cups plain (all-purpose) flour
1 tbs oil
½ tsp salt
2 tbs yoghurt
1 tsp yeast in 2 tbs warm water with a little ginger (ground or fresh)

MATT MUNRO © LONELY PLANET IMAGES. PJFOOD © ALAMY

PUNJAB, INDIA

CHOLE BATURA

Some things are meant to go together: love and marriage, a horse and carriage, and *chole* (tangy, spicy chickpeas) and *batura* (hot, light, puffed-out fried bread).

METHOD

For the chole

1 Heat the oil and fry the chopped onion until pinkish in colour.

2 Add the ginger and garlic and fry for two minutes.

3 Add tomatoes and continue frying. Next, add the chilli, salt, coriander seeds, turmeric and garam masala, then fry for two minutes.

5 Drain the chickpeas and add them to the pan with the tamarind paste and hot water. Let simmer for about 10 minutes, then serve.

For the batura

1 Knead the flour with the other ingredients until smooth. Grease a bowl for the dough, then cover and leave for six hours. When it has risen, knead it again.

2 Make small dough balls and roll out thinly.

3 Heat the oil until very hot and then carefully put in a disc of dough to deep-fry. Use a slotted spoon to press the dough down in the centre of the oil and it should puff out. Remove and eat with *chole*. If it's oily, the oil wasn't hot enough!

TASTING NOTES

In Old Delhi, street food rules. Amid a confusion of streets, stallholders sit behind bubbling cauldrons practising alchemy, at places that specialise in one dish only. To taste Delhi's best *chole batura*, first breathe in the aroma of spicy *chole*, the scents of mingling tamarind, chilli, ginger and coriander. Pay the original owner's grandson and then collect your snack from the servers. It's intensely satisfying to deflate the bread and then use it to wipe up the punchy taste of the chickpeas. The bread alone is a masterpiece: as light as air, a grand puff that is warm to the touch, soft, yet tantalisingly crispy. Alongside it is the *chole*, dark and scented, its fierce spice a foil of perfection. ● *by Abigail Hole*

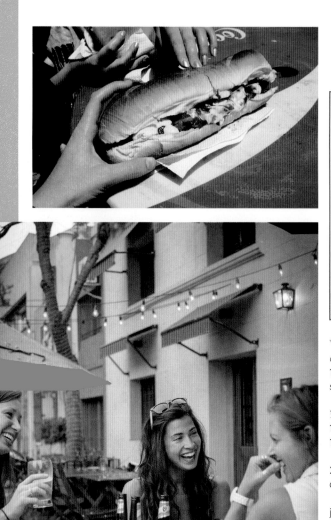

ORIGINS

Though the origins of the *choripán* aren't recorded, the sandwich has been attributed to the gauchos who roamed the landscape several generations ago. In the wide-open grasslands of Patagonia and in the pampas surrounding Buenos Aires, these cowboys were probably the first to grill chorizo and pair it with bread. The sandwich gained popularity in the cities at family *asados*, street carts and sporting events – particularly at raucous *futból* matches, where fans wolf down their *chori* at half-time.

YOU'LL NEED

6 chorizos
1 bunch parsley, chopped
several cloves of garlic, to
    taste, minced
⅓ cup olive oil
1 small tomato, chopped
1 tbs red onion, chopped
    (optional)
2 tbs red wine vinegar
crushed red pepper flakes,
    to taste
juice of ½ lemon or lime
    (optional)
salt
pepper
6 crusty French rolls or one
    baguette

ARGENTINA

CHORIPÁN

A killer combination of chorizo (Spanish-style sausage) and *pan francés* (French bread), *choripán* is the classic sandwich of Argentinian *futból* (soccer) matches, roadside *puestos* (grill carts) and family *asados* (barbecues).

METHOD

1 Place the chorizos on a grill over a medium-high heat.

2 Meanwhile, prepare the chimichurri by combining the parsley, garlic, olive oil, tomato, red onion, red wine vinegar, crushed red pepper flakes and lemon or lime juice in a small bowl. Season with salt and pepper, and add more olive oil, lemon juice or crushed red pepper if desired. It's also possible to combine the ingredients in a food processor, but be sure not to overly process the mixture – the chimichurri should have a slightly chunky texture.

3 Rotate the chorizos on the grill, turning over to grill evenly on each side.

4 Slice the rolls, or cut the baguette into six smaller pieces, then slice.

5 When the chorizos are cooked through and somewhat crisp along the edges, remove from grill.

6 Slice the chorizos lengthwise, and place each one, face up, on a roll. Spoon chimichurri over the chorizo, then close the sandwich. Serve immediately.

TIP *Feel free to be creative with the chimichurri proportions, omitting or adding ingredients where desired –Argentinians serve many variations on the sauce.*

TASTING NOTES

Follow the smoke – and the aroma of sizzling meat – to a *puesto de choripán*, an open-air food cart found at parks and street festivals. The *parrilla*, manned by a no-nonsense *asador* (grillman), will be carefully laid with chorizo, steak and pork – and surrounded by locals listening to *futból* coverage on a radio. Hand over your pesos, then move over to the condiments, where you can top your *chori* with homemade *chimichurri*. Biting into the sandwich, you'll experience an explosion of flavours and textures: the crispy grilled surface of the chorizo, the juicy pork inside, the tangy *chimichurri*, the heat of the garlic, red chilli pepper and onion. Napkins are an advisable accessory. ● *by Bridget Gleeson*

ORIGINS

The centuries-old custom of *cicchetti* is unique to Venice, the magical lagoon that Thomas Mann described as 'half fairy-tale, half tourist trap'. During the 15th century, Venice was the most powerful and wealthiest city in Europe. Its influence (and merchants) brought a diversity of foods to the *bàcari* that lined Venice's *calli* (side streets) and *campi* (plazas), and the worker's tradition of downing a sandwich with a glass of wine persists.

VENICE, ITALY

CICCHETTI

MAKES 15 SLICES

The Venetian answer to tapas, these morsels are found in bars all over Venice and are the perfect salve to an afternoon getting lost amid the city's canals and crowds.

MUSHROOM CROSTINI

YOU'LL NEED

1 baguette, sliced
1 cup mushrooms (dry porcini, fresh shiitake and cremini)
2 tbs extra virgin olive oil
½ onion, minced
1 clove garlic, minced
salt
pepper
1 tbs fresh flat-leaf Italian parsley, roughly chopped
1 tsp lemon zest
grated parmesan cheese, to taste (optional)
1 tbs heavy whipping cream (optional)

METHOD

1 Preheat the oven to 190°C (375°F). Place the baguette slices onto a baking sheet. Toast.

2 Soak the porcini in lukewarm water, then chop the mushrooms together. You can also cube the mushrooms instead of slicing them, if you prefer something more delicate.

3 In a saute pan over medium heat, add the olive oil, then saute the onion and garlic until softened. Add the mushrooms, with salt and pepper to taste. Throw in the parsley. Cook for about 10 minutes until mushrooms have softened, stirring as necessary. If the pan begins to dry out, add more olive oil.

4 Add the lemon zest. Stir (alternatively, you can use a food processor for a more refined spread). Add parmesan cheese. Remove from the heat.

5 Place a spoonful or two of the mushroom mix onto each toasted baguette. If desired, add a shot of cream, then some grated parmesan cheese for added bite. Serve immediately.

TASTING NOTES

To locate an authentic *cicchetti* bar, venture off Venice's crowded streets and keep an eye out for an unassuming storefront thronging with locals during the late morning or afternoon. Fish is a Venetian staple, so you'll often find fried shrimp or calamari, as well as other specialities such as oysters, razor clams, *baccala mantecato* (cod whipped with olive oil) and *sarde in saor* (sardines marinated in vinegar with onions). Other goodies include *polpette* (a fried veal-and-potato meatball), *arancini* (rice balls), zucchini blossoms and baby octopus.

● *by Roger Norum & Strouchan Martins*

ORIGINS

The states edging the Gulf of Mexico have a booming shrimp industry. And since Mexican cuisine has a fine tradition of tweaking foreign food to fit local tastes, it's only natural that when shrimp cocktail was all the rage in the USA in the early 20th century, Mexican chefs put their extra-spicy spin on it. The shrimp is freshest in Veracruz, Tabasco and Campeche, but can be found all over the country, with subtle variations.

YOU'LL NEED

ice
2 cups water or clam juice
700g (1½lb) small shrimp
1 cup ketchup
¼ cup olive oil
juice of 4–6 limes
2 tbs Worcestershire sauce
½ teaspoon freshly ground
  black pepper
salt, to taste
½ cup coriander leaves
  (cilantro), finely chopped
½ cup diced white onion
1 habañero chilli, finely
  chopped (optional)
1 ripe but firm avocado, diced
  (optional)
Mexican-style vinegar-based
  hot sauce
lime wedges
saltine crackers

SERVES 4 AS A GENEROUS APPETISER

MEXICO

COCKTEL DE CAMARÓN

No dreary country-club appetiser here: this shrimp cocktail is a
spicy, sweet-sour treat that capitalises on the freshest seafood.
Slurp it with a spoon, with saltine crackers on the side.

METHOD

1 Fill a medium bowl with ice.

2 Heat water or clam juice to boiling, then add
the shrimp and cook until just pink (less than
one minute). Quickly scoop out the shrimps
and place in the ice. Reserve the cooking
liquid. When the shrimps are cool enough
to handle, peel them and discard the shells.
Refrigerate till chilled.

3 To make the cocktail sauce, combine the
ketchup, olive oil, lime juice, Worcestershire
sauce and pepper, then mix in 1 cup of the
shrimp-cooking liquid. Taste and add salt and/

or more lime juice and cooking liquid if desired
– the mix should be a good balance of salty,
sweet and tangy.

4 Mix in the coriander leaves, onion and chilli
(if using), then gently fold in the avocado,
taking care not to mash the pieces.

5 Divide the cooked shrimp into four parfait
glasses (or other clear glasses). Top with
cocktail sauce and stir gently to combine.

6 Serve with hot sauce, lime wedges and
saltine crackers.

TASTING NOTES

The best way to enjoy *cocktel de camarón* is perched on a plastic chair with your feet in
the sand gazing at the pale green gulf waters. Whether your parfait glass is filled in a proper
kitchen or from a foam cooler, it should be packed with orange-pink shrimp, swimming in
a deep-red sauce, flecked with white onion and green coriander. Along with the lapping
of waves on the shore, a *cocktel* session is marked by the crinkle of cellophane wrappers:
saltine crackers make a fine foil to the intense sauce – and they help if you get a bite spiked
with habañero chilli, a sweat-inducing addition in the Yucatán Peninsula. ● *by Zora O'Neill*

ORIGINS

The native Arawak people of the Bahamas were eating conch long before the arrival of Europeans in the 1500s, but the latter quickly caught on to its usefulness as a quick, high-protein meal and many of today's common conch dishes have remained the same for centuries. Conch is a deeply rooted part of Bahamian culture – old Bahamian dollars feature them, their shells are a standard construction material, and 'Conchy Joe' is a common (though potentially insulting) term for white or mixed-race Bahamians.

SERVES 2 AS
A SNACK

BAHAMAS

CONCH SALAD

In the Bahamas, the conch is a symbol of the nation's resourcefulness, humility and oneness with the ocean, as well as being the star of a tasty salad!

YOU'LL NEED

450g (1lb) conch meat, diced
   into small chunks
1 green pepper, diced
1 white onion, diced
½ cucumber, diced
1 cup diced ripe tomato
2 celery stalks, diced
1 jalapeño chilli, diced
   (optional)
2 garlic cloves, finely chopped
¼ cup lime juice
¼ cup white vinegar
¼ cup orange juice
salt and pepper, to taste

METHOD

Toss all the ingredients together in a large bowl and allow to sit overnight before serving, allowing flavours to mingle.

TASTING NOTES

Though conch is served nearly everywhere in the Bahamas, try to munch the mollusc like the locals do, at a 'fish fry' or 'conch shack'. A fish fry is a sort of outdoor food court, which comes to life on nights and weekends with the crackling of hot oil and the beat of Bahamian goombay music. A conch shack is a roadside or beachfront stall, open daily, serving all manner of conch to travellers and hungry workers alike. At either place, ask for the speciality– some cooks fry legendary conch fritters, while others are known for their zippy conch salad. You can't go wrong with cracked conch, fried to golden brown crispness and served with a creamy orange dipping sauce. ● *by Emily Matchar*

YOU'LL NEED

For the dough
450g (1lb) strong white flour
110g (4oz) lard
100g (3½oz) margarine
¾ cup (175ml) water

For the filling
250g (8¾oz) swede, sliced
200g (7oz) onion, sliced
400g (14oz) beef skirt,
    chunked
600g (1¼lb) potatoes, sliced
black pepper and salt, to
    taste

ORIGINS

Pasties have been munched
since medieval times by people
from all walks of life, but it was
the poor folk of Cornwall who
made pasties their own: by the
end of the 18th century, few
miners or farmers would go to
work without their pastry-
encased lunch. The ingredients
were cheap, the product
portable and the crimped ridge
lifesaving: a disposable grip for
miners working amid high levels
of arsenic. Today, pasty fans
tend to eat the lot.

SERVES 4

CORNWALL, ENGLAND

CORNISH PASTY

Curvaceous (and controversial) pastry parcels, bulging with hearty goodness, these edible lunch boxes of meat and veggies, wrapped in a golden crust, have fed the poor and peckish for centuries.

METHOD

1 Preheat the oven to 220°C (430°F).

2 Rub a quarter of the lard into the flour. Add the remaining lard and the margarine, and stir (with a knife). Add water; stir till absorbed.

3 Knead the dough, then refrigerate for 30 minutes.

4 Divide the pastry into four pieces. On a floured surface, roll each piece into a circle, about 22cm (9in) across.

5 Lay the uncooked swede and onion across each circle's middle; season.

6 Layer on raw meat; season.

7 Add most of the potato; season. Top with the rest of the potato –do not salt.

8 Lightly wet one side of pastry and fold it over the other side, gently pressing together. Crimp the edges to tuck in the contents.

9 Make a cut in the top and brush the top with milk. Bake the pasties for 40–50 minutes, checking halfway through; if browning quickly, turn the oven down to 160°C (320°F).

10 Slice before eating, to release steam.

TASTING NOTES

You can taste the heritage of the Cornish pasty: it's not fancy food, it's fuel. The dense filling – lightly seasoned, best hot – is robust and sustaining. Buying a pasty is an unceremonious affair: you're as likely to find a good one in the village post office as in any artisan deli. Biting into one, pastry melty but firm, slithers of onion caressing tender hunks of beef, is like leaning back into a battered sofa – warm, soft, comforting. Though there's no fish involved (it's thought bad luck to include it), the best place to eat them is by the sea. So take one for a coastal hike – never will a pasty be more deserved, or taste better. ● *by Sarah Baxter*

ORIGINS

In 1949, when Berlin lay in ruins, an enterprising housewife by the name of Herta Heuwer got hold of some curry power from British soldiers. She used this rare ingredient to create a tomato-based curry sauce and slathered it all over chopped sausage. Her stall sat on the outskirts of what was soon to become the red-light district, and the *currywurst* – cheap and filling – became so popular that Heuwer soon opened a small restaurant.

TASTING NOTES

It's been a long night. And that last stein of beer, which seemed such a good idea, has tipped the scales from very merry to downright drunk. As you stumble along, you make out a welcoming beacon of red neon light. The queues are long and rowdy, though there's no hint of aggression. You shuffle forwards, and with each step your whole being is overcome with the scent of sausage, spice and delight. Within minutes, you've mumbled your order and there in the cardboard carton before you are two sausages, chopped up and smothered in a mildly spicy tomato sauce. You stagger home happy, then return the next day to see what it tastes like when sober. It's every bit as good. ● *by Tom Parker Bowles*

GERMANY

CURRYWURST

Currywurst transforms sausage, chopped and doused in a spicy tomato sauce, into night-time nirvana. As you would expect with a German snack, it's the ultimate beer food.

YOU'LL NEED

2 tbs vegetable oil
1 onion, finely diced
2 tbs curry powder
1 tbs hot paprika
2 cups canned tomatoes
½ cup white sugar
¼ cup red wine vinegar
salt and pepper, to taste
5 mild sausages of your
   choice

METHOD

1 Heat the oil in a pan over a medium heat and add the onion, cooking until soft.

2 Add the curry powder and paprika and cook for one minute, then, using your hands, break up the canned tomatoes and add to the mix.

3 Stir in the sugar, vinegar, and salt and pepper to taste. Bring to a boil then reduce to a simmer. Cook until thickened, stirring occasionally. This should take about 25 minutes.

4 Remove from the heat and whizz the sauce in a blender until silky smooth, then strain it through a sieve to remove any pulpiness.

5 Grill the sausages until thoroughly cooked through and nicely browned on the outside. Remove from the heat and slice into 2cm (1in) rounds.

6 Divide the sausage chunks into five bowls and top with a hearty dollop of sauce (re-warmed if necessary). Serve with toothpicks.

ORIGINS

Maize is the very heart of Mexican food, and this is the plant in its most basic form. There's little doubt that early man, and certainly the Aztecs, Incas and the rest of the pre-Columbian indigenous civilisations, feasted upon whole cobs of corn and the smoky, pit-roasted ears remain a staple across Mexico. Like so many other Mexican dishes, *elote* is customised to the eater's personal taste with the modern embellishments of butter, cheese and mayonnaise.

¡Deliciosos!
ELOTES
HERVIDOS,
ASADOS y ESQUITES
= Atendemos Eventos =

SERVES 4

MEXICO

A fresh ear of corn is charred to just-blackened perfection over glowing coals, or simply boiled, then anointed with lime, powdered chilli, butter, cream or cheese.

YOU'LL NEED

4 corn cobs, husks removed
2 tsp fresh lime juice
3 tbs mayonnaise
2 tbs finely grated Parmesan
  cheese
½ tsp chilli powder
¼ tsp ground red pepper
¼ tsp ground cumin
pinch salt

METHOD

1 This one is too easy. Simply grill (broil) or barbecue your corn cobs until they're toasty and tender, making sure they cook evenly on all sides. This should take 10–15 minutes.

2 Meanwhile, combine the lime juice and mayonnaise in one bowl, and all the other ingredients in another.

3 When the corn is done, spread the lime mayo on it and then douse with the spicy cheese mix and devour immediately.

TASTING NOTES

In Mexico, you're never far from corn roasting over coals. The charred, sweetish kernels are fat and hot, redolent of the fire. To eat the cob you can use a stick, or grasp it by the undressed husk. Chilli and lime, that ever-dependable Mexican duo, are all that's needed to complete the feast... And perhaps a splodge of mayonnaise and a handful of grated cheese. Up north, you'll find *elote* boiled, and topped with cream, cheese and chilli powder. This is food to be eaten at a slow amble, an elegant appetiser as you wander through the market, looking for the next course. ● *by Tom Parker Bowles*

ORIGINS

The origin of falafel is the cause for much heated discussion. Arabic, Jewish, Indian, Greek or Turkish – its roots are unclear. The most common theory is that it was eaten by the early Coptic Christians during Lent in Egypt and journeyed across Arabia, where it was a popular way for Muslims to break the fast at Ramadan. Adopted by Mizrahi Jews living in Arab countries, it found its home in Israel in a pita and became the national dish.

YOU'LL NEED

400g (14oz) dried chickpeas (soaked overnight)
4 cups water
5 garlic cloves, minced
½ small onion
½ cup coriander leaves (cilantro), chopped
⅓ cup parsley, chopped
1 tsp paprika
1–2 tsp ground cumin
1 cup breadcrumbs
2 tbs flour
2 tsp bicarb soda (baking soda)
1 egg
2 tsp salt
2 tsp fresh ground pepper
vegetable oil, for deep-frying
1 cup flour, for dipping
4 pita breads
hummus, pesto or chilli sauce (optional)
salad vegetables
tahini (sesame paste)

SERVES 4

ISRAEL

 FALAFEL

Falafel is fast food without any fuss. Simple and affordable, this chickpea ball has been filling bellies in the Middle East for centuries and has rolled all over the world.

METHOD

1 Cook the soaked chickpeas in the water for 30 minutes, drain and put in a food processor (or mash by hand) with the garlic, onion, coriander leaves, parsley and spices. Grind the mixture until you get a rough, juicy consistency; add a little water if needed and more coriander leaves for greener falafel.

2 Pour the mixture into a big bowl. Add the breadcrumbs, flour, bicarb soda, egg, salt and pepper. Stir the mixture well and leave to stand for 30 minutes.

3 Roll the mixture into about 16 small balls and flatten into patties.

4 Heat about 8cm (3in) of vegetable oil in a saucepan. Dip the falafel balls into flour and deep-fry about five at a time until crispy brown (if the falafel crumbles, add more flour to the mixture). When cooked, put the falafel on a paper towel to drain.

5 Stuff four or five falafels into each pita bread along with hummus, salad, tahini or even pesto, and serve hot.

TASTING NOTES

A falafel is a quick snack, but it's also something to be savoured. When ordering, there are important decisions to make, such as whether to add chips, onions, chopped parsley or chilli sauce. Pouring tahini on top is recommended, but not too much in case the bread becomes soggy. It's easy to make a mess while munching on this masterpiece of refreshing salad, tangy pickled cucumbers and smooth, creamy hummus. But the best thing about falafel is that it expands – halfway through you can add more salad fillings. Eventually, all good things come to an end, and at the bottom of the pita you'll find those last fried balls. ● *by Dan Savery Raz*

ORIGINS

The fava bean used for *fuul mudammas* is known in Arabic as *fuul-hammam* due to a quirky medieval business monopoly on production. Having stoked the great fires for Cairo's Princess Public Baths all day, the hammam attendants came up with a great idea: they'd use the leftover embers to slow-cook great vats of *fuul* overnight to be ready for the breakfast rush. Their plan proved a hit, and every morning they had all of Cairo clamouring at their door.

YOU'LL NEED

For the broad beans

7 cups water
2 cups dried broad beans (fava beans), soaked for 24 hours, then drained and rinsed (or use 4 cups canned cooked beans instead)

For the fuul

1 onion, finely diced
3–4 garlic cloves, finely chopped
1 tomato, finely chopped
⅛ cup squeezed lemon juice
½ tsp cumin
½ tsp chilli powder
pinch of turmeric
pinch of cayenne pepper
pinch of cinnamon
salt
pepper
olive oil, to taste
pita bread
hard-boiled eggs (optional)
feta (optional)
parsley
tomatoes
cucumber

TASTING NOTES

Wafts of garlic hang over the street. Members of the swelling crowd are clutching empty containers. Squeeze your way up to the front, where the vendor is working up a sweat and the customers are yelling with impatience. You're handed a pita sandwich, spread with a generous dollop of *fuul* and garnished with fresh salad. The first bite reveals the soft, comforting texture of beans and olive oil. As you chew, the tart zing of lemon, the peppery taste of cumin and the powerful punch of garlic come into play. It's hearty and wholesome, and surprisingly filling. Your pita is finished. You look at the crowd and nod at their intelligence. Next time you're bringing a pot to fill too. ● *by Jessica Lee*

EGYPT

FUUL MUDAMMAS

SERVES 4

Egypt's breakfast of champions is the country's national dish.
Served up as a sandwich filler, this spice-fest of a broad bean (fava
bean) stew keeps the 80-million-strong population on the move.

METHOD

For the broad beans

1 In a large pot bring the water to the boil.

2 Add the fava beans and boil for 10–15 minutes, making sure to skim any foam off the top.

3 Reduce heat, cover the pot and simmer for eight hours.

4 After simmering for eight hours, check for dryness. If too dry, add boiling water to the pot.

5 Cover and cook on a low heat for another two hours.

TIP *You can skip this step by using canned beans.*

For the fuul

1 In a large frying pan, saute the diced onion until translucent.

2 Add the garlic and fry on a low heat for 2–3 minutes.

3 Add the tomato to the pan and fry for another 5 minutes.

4 Transfer the frying-pan mix to the pot of broad beans.

5 Stir in the lemon juice, all the spices and seasonings and olive oil.

6 Cook over a low heat for 15–20 minutes.

7 Mash the mixture using a potato masher to a consistency of your liking (or for a less chunky version put it in a blender until smooth).

8 Serve in bowls (drizzled with extra olive oil) with pita bread, hard-boiled eggs, chunks of feta, and a salad of parsley, tomatoes and cucumber for an authentic Egyptian breakfast.

TIP *Swap and change the seasoning measurements to suit your tastes.*

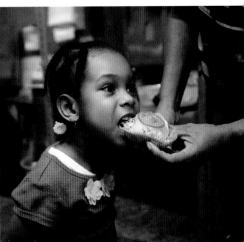

ORIGINS

It's no surprise that Central America's most culturally diverse nation should produce a dish with Mayan, Mestizo and Caribbean roots topped with old-European flavour. Corn and beans are common in Central America and Mexico, while an onion and pepper mixture would be equally welcome on Maya, Creole or Garifuna tables. But what makes this dish distinctly Belizean is the *garnache*'s signature sharp cheese, produced by the nation's Mennonite farmers.

MAKES 12 TORTILLAS

BELIZE

GARNACHES

Though 'tasty things spread on fried corn' is a broad street food category indeed, the tangy mixture of beans, onions, peppers and sharp cheese collectively known as *garnaches* is distinctly Belizean.

YOU'LL NEED

1 cup onion, freshly diced
2 spicy habanera peppers, finely chopped
1 cup white distilled vinegar
¼ tsp salt
12 corn tortillas
black beans (canned or freshly made), blended, but not so much as to be runny.
110g (4oz) Asiago or Parmesan cheese, grated

METHOD

1 Prepare the onion and pepper mixture by combining them with the salt and distilled vinegar in a jar, and leaving it to sit for anywhere from an hour to a day.

2 Spread a few tablespoons of the black bean mixture on a tortilla.

3 Sprinkle the grated cheese over the beans.

4 Spoon a tablespoon or so of the onion-pepper mixture over the top.

5 Not spicy enough? Try a dash of Marie Sharp's hot sauce, if an extra kick is needed.

TASTING NOTES

The *garnache*'s fried corn tortilla is crisp and warm, neither greasy nor stale, especially when freshly made. The black bean mixture is thinner than your average refried beans, but thicker than a soup. Topping this, a tangy onion mixture made with chopped onion and habanera peppers steeped in vinegar. Every stall in Belize has its own unique blend! Most unique is the sharp Mennonite-produced cheese melted perfectly between the beans and onions. Belizeans call this 'Dutch cheese', and it's best described as a cross between Asiago and Parmesan. Last (but not least), a dash of Marie Sharp's Hot Sauce, without which no dish in Belize would be considered complete. ● *by Joshua Samuel Brown*

YOU'LL NEED

2 cups white rice, cooked and kept warm in the pot
1 bundle spinach
½ carrot, julienned into long, thin strips
5 crab sticks
3 eggs, beaten
1 *takuan* (pickled daikon radish)
5 sheets *nori* (seaweed paper)
olive oil, for frying
sesame oil, for brushing
salt, to season

For the rice seasoning
1 tbs sesame oil
1 tbs sesame seed
1 tsp salt

TASTING NOTES

Gimbap is the ultimate on-the-go food in Korea, sold at convenience stores and street stalls, as it can be nibbled upon virtually anywhere. There's nothing quite like washing down *gimbap* with a cold beer whilst watching the Korean countryside pass by from a train. Crunch through the crisp seaweed exterior and an explosion of flavours flows forth – savoury, salty and spicy from pickles and *kimchi*. The inclusion of mayo, radish or sometimes crab meat (unlike Japanese maki, *gimbap* never contains raw fish) provides a sweet counterpoint to the affair. Perfect sticky rice helps make the experience both filling and moreish: you might not need more than one serving, but you'll definitely want it. *by Megan Eaves*

SERVES 2–3

SOUTH KOREA

GIMBAP

**A colourful rainbow of ingredients is essential to a Korean
gimbap, which has a mouth-tingling kick thanks to the addition
of Korea's national dish: *kimchi* (spicy fermented cabbage).**

METHOD

To prepare

1 Blanch the spinach for 10 seconds. Rinse with cold water, drain and set aside.

2 Stir-fry the carrot strips in a hot pan with olive oil and a dash of salt. Set aside.

3 Heat a glug of olive oil in a small frying pan and add the eggs so they cover the whole pan in a thick layer. Season, cook through, then remove from the heat. When cooled, slice into long strips. Set aside.

4 Grill the crab meat for 2–3 minutes. Slice into long strips, then set aside.

5 Slice the pickled daikon into long strips.

To roll

1 Transfer the cooked rice into a large bowl. Gently mix in the sesame oil, sesame seeds and salt. Leave to cool for 5–10 minutes. The rice should be warm but not hot, as steam may break the seaweed paper.

2 Cover a bamboo sushi-rolling mat with plastic wrap. Lay one piece of nori on the mat lengthwise; spread the rice evenly on top, leaving 1cm (0.4in) of each end of the paper rice-free.

3 Tightly stack several strips of each ingredient widthways on the end of the roll closest to you.

4 Start rolling slowly from the end closest to you. As you go, press and squeeze to keep the shape tight.

5 When you reach the end of the roll, lightly wet the edge of the seaweed paper with water and press it onto the roll to seal it.

6 Apply a light layer of sesame oil to the surface of the roll.

7 Slice the gimbap into 6–8 rounds with a very sharp knife.

YOU'LL NEED

5¼ cups plain (all-purpose)
  flour
2½ tsp salt
2 tsp dried yeast powder
1 tsp sugar
1¼ cups water
1 cup spinach, chopped
1 cup feta cheese, crumbled
½ cup vegetable oil
5 tbs butter
lemon wedges, to serve

ORIGINS

Savoury-dough pastries date
back thousands of years in
Turkey. Originally from rural
Turkey, *gözleme* migrated to
the cities to serve as fast food
for traders and market-goers.
Today, it's common to see
gözleme vendors sitting in
markets and shop windows
cooking on large round griddles
called *sacs*. In more recent
years, *gözleme* have become
a popular snack in places as
far-flung as Germany and
Australia.

TURKEY

GÖZLEME

MAKES 10

Dubbed 'Turkish crepes' by some, these stuffed flatbreads are
served fresh in Turkey's many outdoor markets – watching
them being made is almost as much fun as eating them!

SPINACH & CHEESE GÖZLEME

METHOD

1 Sift the flour into a bowl, reserving 1 cup of flour. Add the salt.

2 Combine the yeast and sugar in another bowl, add ¼ cup of water and stir.

3 Make a well in the centre of the flour, and pour the liquid into the hole, covering the top with some flour. Allow to rise for 10 minutes.

4 Add the rest of the water, stirring thoroughly. Knead the mixture for about five minutes, then cover and allow to rise until it has doubled in size (about one hour).

5 Toss the spinach and feta cheese together in a medium bowl; set aside.

6 Put the dough on a lightly floured surface, then divide it into 10 equal portions. Shape each portion into a ball, and roll each ball with a rolling pin until it forms a rectangle slightly less than 5mm (¼in) thick.

7 Brush the surface with oil. Fold the opposite edge of each square together, bringing the edges together in the centre.

8 Sprinkle the feta and spinach mixture on half the dough, then fold the other half over to form an oval shape. Seal the edges well by pressing gently.

9 Heat a griddle or heavy frying pan and grease the surface with butter. Put the *gözleme* on the griddle and cook until the surface is lightly speckled with brown spots (the 'eyes'). Serve hot, with lemon wedges.

TASTING NOTES

Gözleme is the ideal street snack to keep you energised for shopping for spices, lamps and all the other things that make Turkish markets so seductive. Look out for vendors bent over a circular griddle, cooking up what looks like an oversized crepe. The vendors fold the pancakes as delicately as origami, browning them on the griddle then chopping them into squares. Whatever the filling – spinach and cheese, minced lamb, spiced eggplant – the *gözleme* are delectable, their flaky dough yielding to the soft interior. Bite into one, and suddenly American-style fast food seems about as appealing as eating a wet sock.

● *By Emily Matchar*

YOU'LL NEED

1½ tsp sweet paprika
3 tbs sea salt
¼ tsp pepper
¼ tsp ground oregano
1.1kg (2½lb) boneless pork loin
white wine vinegar

For the tzatziki sauce

2 medium cucumbers,
    peeled, seeded and diced
1 tbs salt
1 garlic clove, chopped
1 tbs fresh dill, finely chopped
2 tbs lemon juice
3 cups Greek yoghurt

To serve

6–8 pieces of pocketless pita
    bread
olive oil
tzatziki sauce or plain Greek
    yoghurt
2 tomatoes, sliced
1 medium onion, sliced
salt, to taste
freshly ground black pepper,
    to taste

ORIGINS

The name gyros comes from
Greek γύρος (turn), which is
a calque of the Turkish word
döner; it was originally called
ντονέρ (do'ner) in Greece too.
İskender Efendi of Bursa in
Turkey claims to have invented
the vertical grilling technique
in the 1860s, improving on the
ancient horizontal method.
Gyros was brought to Greece in
the 1920s by refugees from Asia
Minor. Gyros is typically made
with pork and seasoned with a
distinct spice mix.

GREECE

GYROS

Pronounced 'yee-ross', this pita wrap stuffed with hot, greasy slices of spit-roast marinated meat and dripping with delicious garlicky sauce makes a perfectly satisfying late-night snack.

METHOD

1 Combine the paprika, salt, pepper and oregano in a small bowl.

2 Slice the pork as thinly as possible, then pound to less than 5mm (¼in) thick.

3 Arrange some of the meat slices to cover the bottom of a flat-bottomed dish, then sprinkle with the spice mixture and enough vinegar so that all the pieces are moistened. Continue layering meat, spices and vinegar until all the meat has been seasoned. Cover and leave to marinate in the refrigerator for at least two hours. While the meat is marinating, prepare the tzatziki sauce.

4 Cut the marinated meat into strips about 1cm (½in) wide and 5cm (2in) long.

5 Cook in a very hot nonstick frying pan until the meat is browned and slightly crisp.

6 Brush the pita with a thin layer of olive oil and grill until it is warm but not crisp. Arrange the meat on the pita and top it with tzatziki sauce (see below) or yoghurt, a few tomato slices, sliced onion, and salt and black pepper, to taste. Roll your pita, wrap it in waxed paper, and serve.

For the tzatziki sauce

1 In a colander, sprinkle the cucumbers with 1 tbs salt and allow them to drain for at least 30 minutes. Rinse and pat dry with paper towel.

2 Combine the cucumbers, garlic, dill and lemon juice, and puree in a blender or food processor.

3 Stir this mixture into the Greek yoghurt, and allow to rest in the refrigerator for at least two hours to allow the flavours to develop.

TASTING NOTES

In Greek cities, you're never far from a *souvlatzidiko*, where the aroma of seasoned pork, chicken or beef draws crowds. If the smell isn't enough to get you interested, the sight of the stacks of slow-roasting meat surely will be. Onions, tomatoes and tzatziki sauce are the most common toppings, but it's not unusual to find yoghurt, fried potatoes, lettuce and green pepper on offer as well. It takes both hands to hold a stuffed gyros sandwich, wrapped in waxed paper and the all-important napkin; gyros can be messy, the pita scarcely containing the meat's juices. ● *by Meredith Snyder*

YOU'LL NEED

For the chicken

1 whole chicken (1.8kg, 3½lb)
salt
10cm (4in) fresh ginger, peeled and thinly sliced
3 spring onions, cut into 2cm (1in) sections
250g (½lb) pork bones (optional)
1 tbs sesame oil

For the rice

2 cups jasmine rice
2 tbs vegetable oil
2cm (1in) section of ginger, peeled and minced
3 medium cloves garlic, minced
½ tsp sesame oil

2 cups broth from poaching the chicken
1 tsp salt

For the chilli sauce

6 hot red chillies, chopped
1 shallot, chopped
2 tbs fresh ginger, peeled and chopped
2 medium garlic cloves, minced
½ tsp salt
⅓ cup fresh lime juice

To serve

¼ cup dark soy sauce
a few sprigs coriander leaves (cilantro)
1 cucumber, thinly sliced
1 bunch watercress

TASTING NOTES

Take your time, and ask around. Every stall has a slightly different version; you might get lucky and stumble upon the greatest one of them all. You're looking for every element to work on its own, and then to combine and create something greater than the sum of its parts. The chicken should be alabaster white, and lusciously tender and silken; too dry, and the whole thing's ruined. The rice is laced with garlic and ginger. The dish is served accompanied by cucumber, soy sauce and a chilli-garlic paste that should neither under- nor overwhelm. The broth is served on the side, delicate but sustaining. Once you've tried the real thing, you'll know what this dish is all about. ● *by Tom Parker Bowles*

MALAYSIA & SINGAPORE

HAINANESE CHICKEN RICE

Described by many as the 'national dish' of Singapore, this seemingly simple bowl of slow-poached chicken and rice in a delicate broth is as comforting as a warm embrace.

METHOD

1 Season the chicken with salt inside and out. Stuff with the ginger slices and spring onion.

2 Place the chicken and optional pork bones in a large stockpot and fill with water to cover by about 2cm (1in). Bring to a boil over high heat, then lower the heat to a simmer. Cook for about 30 minutes till a thermometer inserted into the thickest part of the thigh reads 75ºC (170ºF) and the juices of the flesh under the leg run clear.

3 Remove from the heat and transfer the chicken to a bowl of ice water. Discard the ginger and spring onion but reserve the poaching broth. The quick cooling keeps the chicken meat and skin firm and tender.

4 Wash the rice, then soak it in cool water for at least 10 minutes. Drain.

5 In a large saucepan, heat the vegetable oil over medium-high heat. When hot, add the ginger and garlic and saute for a few minutes. Pour the rice and sesame oil into the saucepan, stir to coat and cook for about two minutes.

6 Add 2 cups of the reserved poaching broth, and salt to taste. Bring to a boil then turn the heat to low, cover the saucepan tightly and cook for 15 minutes. Remove from the heat and leave it to sit (with the lid still on) for five to ten minutes more.

7 While the rice is cooking, remove the chicken from the ice water and rub it with the sesame oil. Carve the chicken for serving.

8 Blend the chilli sauce ingredients in a food processor until smooth.

9 Reheat the remaining broth, add salt to taste and serve on the side with the other condiments and garnishes.

ORIGINS

In the 14th century, Willem Beuckelszoon revolutionised herring consumption with the invention of gibbing, an alchemy of salt, fish entrail enzymes and oak casks. The resulting portable protein helped fuel the Dutch merchant ships along the world's trade routes. Today, *Hollandse Nieuwe* season remains a huge event in the Netherlands, with live news coverage of the first haul and happy herring-eaters bingeing in the streets.

THE NETHERLANDS

HOLLANDSE NIEUWE HARING

As street food goes, raw, lightly brined herring is a bit drab, even unappetising. But one bite reveals its secret: this is silky, impeccably fatty essence of the sea.

BROODJE HARING

YOU'LL NEED

1 *Hollandse Nieuwe* herring
small bread roll (what the Dutch call a pistolet)
1 tbs white onion, finely chopped
3 slices of cucumber pickle

METHOD

Fresh *Hollandse Nieuwe* herring gets exported to fishmongers in the know in early June. Otherwise, you'll have to head to Holland to get proper raw herring. To make your own sandwich, lay one whole, cleaned herring in the roll (slice the tail off if you prefer), then top with the onion and pickle. That's it – the Dutch are the masters of the minimalist sandwich.

TASTING NOTES

Hollandse Nieuwe kiosks dot main squares and sit at the tops of canal bridges, handy for cycling customers. A good vendor will deftly clean and fillet each fish as it's ordered, and in Amsterdam, the fillets are chopped into bite-size squares and served on a small cardboard plate with a toothpick trimmed with a miniature Dutch flag. Each morsel – grey on the outside, but a luscious pink inside – is lightly salty and almost melt-in-your-mouth soft with fat; the optional onion and pickles help off set the richness. Once you're *haring*-savvy, you'll see the stalls everywhere, even at the airport, where a pit stop can instantly revive your brain after a red-eye –thanks, omega-3 fatty acids. ● *by Zora O'Neill*

ORIGINS

Though sausages have been around since the 9th century BC, it took late-19th-century German-American immigrants to slap one in a bun and call it a hot dog. The name may have come from the sausage's resemblance to dachshunds, but the exact origins are unknown. First sold at fairs and baseball games, hot dogs rose to iconic status with the 1916 founding of Nathan's Famous hot dog stand at Coney Island in Brooklyn, New York.

SERVES 4

USA

HOT DOG

Indelibly associated with baseball, carnivals and backyard parties, this humble boiled or grilled sausage served in a soft roll and topped with condiments is the unofficial food of American summer.

YOU'LL NEED

4 kosher beef hot dogs
4 hot-dog buns (poppy seed buns are best)
yellow mustard
1 white onion, diced
jar of pickled medium-hot peppers (in Chicago, these are usually called 'sport peppers' – in other parts of the world you can substitute chopped pepperoncini or jarred pickled tabasco peppers)
2 tomatoes, cut into wedges
dill pickle spears, to taste
sweet pickle relish, to taste
celery salt, to taste

METHOD

1 In a pot or Dutch oven fitted with a steamer rack or bamboo steamer basket, boil about 10cm (4in) of water (the water should remain below the level of the steamer rack).

2 Reduce the heat to low, place the hot dogs atop the steamer rack, cover the pot and simmer for about four minutes.

3 Carefully open the pot and place the buns on top of the hot dogs to steam for a further two minutes.

4 Carefully remove the buns and hot dogs with a pair of tongs.

5 To assemble, place the hot dogs in the buns, top with mustard, onion, peppers, tomato wedges, pickle spears and pickle relish to taste, then sprinkle with celery salt.

TASTING NOTES

Imagine it's a summer evening at the baseball stadium. At the 7th inning stretch, you make your way to the hot-dog stand. The vendor hands you your dog, wrapped in a silver jacket. Immediately, you roll back the foil and bite in. The meat is hot and salty, perfumed with garlic, its juices dripping into the absorbent bun. Condiments – ketchup, mustard, sauerkraut, pickle relish – cut the fattiness. One, two, three, four bites, and it is gone. You line up and do it all over again.

This recipe is for Chicago-style dogs, which are typically served up so veggie-laden that they're described as being 'dragged through the garden'. ● *by Emily Matchar*

AMIEL, JEAN-CLAUDE © GETTY IMAGES, SIVAN ASKAYO, KRIS DAVIDSON © LONELY PLANET IMAGES

YOU'LL NEED

3 medium onions, finely
  chopped
1 garlic bulb, finely chopped
6 sliced scotch bonnet
  chillies (you can substitute
  jalapeños)
2 tbs fresh thyme
2 tbs ground allspice
2 tbs sugar
2 tbs salt
2 tsp ground black pepper
1–2 tsp ground cinnamon
1–2 tsp nutmeg
1–2 tsp ginger
½ cup olive oil
½ cup soy sauce
1 lime, juiced
1 cup orange juice
1 cup white vinegar
1.5kg (about 3lb) boneless
  pork loin

ORIGINS

Pork was the original jerk meat,
a leftover from the Spanish
conquest, along with the
Maroons – African slaves left
to fend for themselves on the
islands. The Maroons needed
meat that could be easily
transported, so they came up
with a jerk seasoning made from
local ingredients that had the
bonus of flavouring the meat
when smoked over pimento
wood fires. This fugitive's meal
soon became a finger-licking-
good part of Caribbean culture.

JAMAICA & CARIBBEAN ISLANDS

JERKED PORK

Pork, marinated in Scotch bonnet chillies, allspice, sugar, cinnamon and a plethora of other ingredients, is slow-cooked over a smoky woodfire to create this dish, best eaten with the fingers.

METHOD

1 Roughly chop the onions, garlic and chillies. Put them in a blender with all the other ingredients (except the pork) and blend until you have a smooth sauce.

2 Put the pork in a deep dish and, using a fork or paring knife, make small holes in the meat so the marinade can really soak in. Pour about a cup of marinade over the meat and massage it in.

3 Cover and leave to marinate – preferably overnight, but five hours will do if you're pressed for time.

4 Take the meat out of the fridge and let it come back to room temperature for about half an hour, before putting it on the grill (you could also bake this in a medium oven if it's easier).

5 Baste it regularly with the leftover marinade. It should take a little under three hours to cook, so baste it and turn it every 20–30 minutes. The end result should be sticky and dark (because of the sugar).

6 Allow the meat to rest for about half an hour before slicing.

TIP *Make sure to wash your hands very thoroughly after rubbing the marinade into the pork – the chillies pack some serious heat!*

TASTING NOTES

You'll have no problem spotting the jerk stalls, surrounded as they are in billowing clouds of exquisitely scented smoke. The cooking vehicle of choice is usually a split oil barrel, the coals expertly tended. Pimento wood is less common now, and the smoking of the meat pretty much extinct. Still, the jerk seasoning varies from stall to stall. The meat should be tender and bursting with juice; the heat comes first, a fruity chilli blast, then a sweetness to temper the fire. Each bite should have a whisper of allspice, and a hint of nutmeg or cinnamon. And the crust... Oh, that crust: blackened and sticky, containing the quintessence of the jerk. One portion is never enough. ● *by Tom Parker Bowles*

ORIGINS

The conquistadors and the Incas would have been fans of the *juane* since its simple preparation method meant it was ideal for long-haul boat journeys and it made use of readily available ingredients. It's not clear when the *juane* first became identifiable with John the Baptist (San Juan Bautista) but thus is the name derived: the leaf-wrapped goodie bags are synonymous with the San Juan festival, celebrated across the Peruvian jungle on 24 June.

YOU'LL NEED

For the garlic paste
450g (about 1lb) garlic
½ cup olive oil
pinch of salt
pepper, to taste
grating of *guizador* root (or fresh turmeric)

For the leaf & filling
2 *bijao* leaf (if unavailable, substitute with banana leaf)

1 cup rice (white rice is best, but brown rice works too)
2 medium chicken breast, diced into chunky segments
4 garlic cloves
2 tsp oregano
2 tsp cumin
pinch of turmeric
2–3 bay leaves
pinch of salt
pepper, to taste
handful of pitted black olives
1 egg

TASTING NOTES

There's something about rice compacted in 'cake' format that enhances the eating experience. Imagine, then, what wonders whisking the rice with egg, black olives, garlicky chicken and a medley of spices and squeezing it together in a leaf that secretes its juices into the rice, can do. Having to unwrap your *juane* like a present before you can consume it adds to the magic. Then there are those few seconds while you wait to peel back the leaves and chow down, when the aroma of tender chicken and freshly mown grass hits the air and magnifies that pit in your stomach. Yes, technically *juane* is more river than street food, but when you taste it, you'll let us off ... ● *by Luke Waterson*

AMAZON BASIN, PERU

JUANE

Prepare for that long Amazon boat journey as rainforest farmers and fishermen have for centuries, with this concoction of chicken, rice and spices wrapped in a jungle leaf.

METHOD

1 Make a garlic paste by topping and tailing the garlic, and placing in a baking dish covered in the olive oil. Sprinkle with salt and pepper, and grate in the guizador root. Cover the dish and bake for 45 minutes, then remove the cover and bake for a further 15 minutes until the garlic is brown.

2 Separate the cloves and in a separate bowl gently squeeze them out of their skins. Pour in the oil from the baking dish and blend in a food processor. Cool the paste, then refrigerate it.

3 Ideally, heat the *bijao* leaf over an open flame to improve its elasticity, then wipe it clean.

4 Cook the rice until it is slightly underdone.

5 Meanwhile, amply baste the chicken segments in the garlic paste (you do not have to use all the paste). Cook the chicken in olive oil in a frying pan on the hob, turning repeatedly.

6 When the rice is done, ensure it is broken up so that there are no clumps, and mix it with the juices from the cooked chicken.

7 Saute the garlic cloves in a little oil in a frying pan and add to the rice mixture. Add the oregano, cumin, tumeric and bay leaves and season to taste.

8 Stir the handful of olives into the rice and spice mixture.

9 Beat the egg into the rice, and mix well.

10 Put a scoop of the rice mixture along with some chicken segments in each *bijao* leaf and tie each firmly with string to leave a 'neck'.

11 Boil the *juanes* in a large pot of water for one hour. Serve immediately.

ORIGINS

Some claim that the *kati* roll was invented as a portable *tiffin* (light lunch) for Bengali office workers. Others insist that the dish was cooked up for colonial sahibs too fastidious to get their hands dirty while eating. Either way, the first *kati* rolls trundled out of the kitchens of Nizam's Restaurant in Kolkata in the 1930s; once word got out, there was no stopping them. Today, hole-in-the-wall takeaways are feted like Michelin-star restaurants for their *kati* rolls.

YOU'LL NEED

For the kati *kebabs*
1 tsp ground cumin
1 tsp ground chilli
½ tsp lemon juice
1½ tsp ground coriander seeds
1 clove garlic, crushed
½ tsp pepper
½ tsp ground ginger
1 tbs canola oil
salt, to taste
400g (14oz) minced (ground) lamb

For the parathas
2 cups *atta* (wholewheat flour)
½ tsp salt
1 cup water
½ cup ghee

For the kati *rolls*
1 onion, chopped
2 green chillies, chopped
parathas
1 egg, beaten
kati kebabs
garlic-and-chilli sauce

TIP *To spice up your parathas, fold mashed potato, chopped coriander leaves (cilantro), cumin seed and chilli into the dough before you roll it out.*

KOLKATA, INDIA

KATI ROLL

SERVES 8

**Is it a kebab? Is it a wrap? A souped-up sandwich?
A powered-up *paratha* (fried flatbread)? Enter the *kati*
roll – Kolkata's favourite portable snack!**

METHOD

For the kati *kebabs*

1 Grind the spices and other ingredients into a paste, then mix together with the minced lamb, and marinate for about four hours.

2 Form the mixture into long sausage shapes and press on to metal skewers.

3 Grill the kebabs over hot charcoal, or in a hot oven, turning regularly and brushing with extra oil to seal in the flavour.

For the parathas

1 Make a dough with the flour, salt and water.

2 Take egg-sized balls of dough and rub them with ghee, then set them aside for 30 to 45 minutes.

3 Roll the balls of dough into flat sheets, then heat on a tava or hotplate for about 45 seconds on each side, until brown spots appear. Brush with a little extra ghee on each side during the cooking process to crisp up the paratha. Set aside.

For the kati *rolls*

1 Saute the onion and chilli in a wok or frying pan until the onion begins to turn transparent.

2 Brush one side of each paratha with the beaten egg, cook until the egg sets, then remove from the heat.

3 Place in the middle of each paratha the onions and chilli, a *kati* kebab, and a squeeze of garlic-and-chilli sauce. Roll tightly and serve.

TASTING NOTES

During the evening rush hour, when office workers gather for their nightly fix, you'll see vendors rolling this portable feast at breakneck speed. Sizzle, seal, wrap and deliver, sizzle, seal, wrap and deliver, then on to the next customer in seconds flat. The flavours are rich, fragrant and immediate. The softness of the paratha gives way to the tender meat within, and each bite delivers a crunch of chilli and onion and a swoosh of sauce and spices. *Kati* rolls should be eaten fresh off the *tava* (griddle) when the paratha is hot and the sauces and meat juices are still mingling. Vegetarians can get in on the act with *kati* rolls filled with spiced egg, potato and paneer. ● *by Joe Bindloss*

ORIGINS

Nowadays *kelewele* (keleh-weleh) is fried up all over Ghana, but it's originally a food of the Ga people, from Accra and the country's south-eastern coast. The snack was created to use plantains that were going bad: the chilli masked the overripe taste, the ginger warded off nausea, while the frying firmed them up. But not to worry: today's *kelewele* is made with plantains just ripe enough to be sweet, soft and delicious.

SERVES 2
AS
A SNACK

GHANA

A sublime combination of sweet plantain tossed with
salt, ginger and fresh chilli, *kelewele* is like the spicy,
plantain version of french fries, only better.

YOU'LL NEED

1 cup vegetable oil
2 ripe plantains, sliced into
  thin strips
2 tbs minced ginger
1 minced chilli (or a little more
  or less, to taste)
½ tsp salt

METHOD

1 Heat the vegetable oil in a small saucepan.

2 Toss the sliced plantains in a bowl with the ginger, chilli and salt; marinate for a few minutes.

3 Fry the plantain strips in the oil until golden brown.

TASTING NOTES

Kelewele is served after the heat of the day has faded. The street-food scene is happening: people are taking walks, and roadside stalls are lit with lamps. The *kelewele* stall is popular with everyone, but especially couples (it's a traditional first-date food) and pregnant women (*kelewele* is supposed to be beneficial). When the *kelewele*'s ready, the heat – and some of the oil – seeps through the newspaper that holds it, and no one can wait until it cools to dig in. The crunchy plantain is spicy and sweet, the flavours of ginger and plantain playing off each other, and the heat of the chilli builds with each bite until it burns. The aftertaste is sweetness and pure fire. ● *by Amy Karafin, with Barbara Sarpong*

2–3 cups vegetable oil, plus
   2 tbs, for frying
2½ tbs red curry paste
1 tsp curry powder
½ tsp ground turmeric
1 tsp ground cardamom
   (optional)
3 cups unsweetened coconut
   milk
1½–2kg (3–4lb) chicken, cut
   into 6 pieces
1¾ cups chicken stock
1 tsp sugar
2 tbs fish sauce, or more to
   taste
700g (1½lb) fresh egg noodles
   or 350g (¾lb) dried
2–6 dried red chillies
⅓ cup shallots, thinly sliced
¾ cup Chinese pickled
   mustard greens, chopped
1 lime, cut into wedges
handful coriander leaves
   (cilantro), chopped
⅓ cup spring onions, chopped

ORIGINS

Khao soi is thought to have
roots in Myanmar (Burma),
where Chinese Muslims from
Yunnan province brought an
early version down to Thailand
and Laos. Originally said to be
halal (so, pork free), it now can
contain pork, as well as the
more usual beef and chicken.
Curry paste was added later,
along with coconut milk, to
create a rich, reasonably spicy
dish that is enjoyed mainly in the
afternoon and evening.

TASTING NOTES

If you're lucky, the noodles might still be made manually, with the wheat ground, boiled,
stretched and sliced by hand. What you want in the dish is balance: spice, but not so much it
overpowers; coconut milk, added in just the right amount so it doesn't overwhelm and make
everything dull and overly sweet. The meat should be cooked in the broth, the noodles soft
and chewy. The deep-fried noodles on top should shatter between the teeth. Oh, and that
pickled cabbage is essential: it adds a welcome sour note, along with the lime. Sit down at
the rickety table, and slurp and sip to your heart's content. *Khao soi* satisfies every eating
urge. ● *by Tom Parker Bowles*

SERVES 4

NORTHERN THAILAND

KHAO SOI

Chiang Mai's signature dish is a creamy, spicy Thai comfort curry with noodles two ways and a side order of zesty pickled cabbage.

METHOD

1 Heat 2 tbs of the oil in a large, heavy saucepan over medium heat then add the red curry paste, curry powder, turmeric and optional cardamom. Cook, stirring constantly for about two minutes.

2 Add one cup of the coconut milk and bring to a boil, stirring well for about two minutes. Add one more cup of coconut milk, return to a boil, and again boil for about two minutes.

3 Add the chicken pieces, one cup of chicken stock and remaining coconut milk then bring to a boil again. Simmer and thin the broth as needed with chicken stock or water.

4 Add the sugar and fish sauce. Cover and simmer for about 45 minutes.

5 If you're using dried noodles, cook all the noodles in a large pot of boiling water, stirring well till they are tender but firm, about seven minutes or more. If you're using fresh noodles, set aside one cup, then boil the rest till tender and firm, about three minutes. Drain and rinse well in cold water then add a dash of oil and mix well to prevent the noodles from sticking together. If you used dried noodles, set aside one cup of the noodles and dry them with a clean dishtowel.

6 Heat the remaining oil in a large saucepan over medium-high heat. Place the cup of towel-dried noodles or the cup of uncooked fresh noodles into the saucepan a few strands at a time. Fry them, turning once, until crisp and golden. Remove from the heat and set aside. Add the dried chillies to the pan and fry for a few seconds until they puff up; set aside.

7 Divide the remaining boiled noodles into four bowls. Ladle the chicken curry over the noodles and top with shallots, mustard greens, fried noodles, lime wedges, fried chillies, coriander leaves and spring onion, and serve.

YOU'LL NEED

2 cups plain (all-purpose)
  flour
1 tsp baking powder
½ tsp salt
2 eggs
2 tbs water
2 tbs oil
2 cups onions, finely diced
salt and pepper, to taste
2 cups mashed potatoes
1 extra egg, beaten with 1 tsp
  water, for an egg wash

ORIGINS

The knish came to New York
with the Ashkenazi Jews of
Eastern Europe. It's a form of
piroshki, but in the early days,
when it was sold from stalls as
a hot lunch for workmen, the
meat disappeared to make it
more economical. But as money
returned, so did the filling of
chopped liver and various kinds
of meat, and today the contents
of this carb-heavy pastry vary
from store to store.

MAKES 8

NEW YORK, USA

KNISH

Seriously sustaining, the knish is a hefty, round pastry usually filled with mashed potato or buckwheat groats (kasha), along with sauerkraut, onions, meat or cheese, wrapped in pastry, then baked.

METHOD

1 Combine the flour, baking powder and salt in a large bowl. Make a well in the centre of the flour (imagine you're looking down into a volcano) and pour the eggs, 2 tbsp of water and 1 tbsp of oil into it. Mix everything together gently until a dough is formed.

2 Knead the dough on a lightly floured surface until it is smooth, then place it in a bowl brushed with oil. Cover it and let it stand for an hour.

3 Preheat the oven to 180°C (350°F).

4 In a frying pan, cook the onions in the remaining oil until softened, then season with salt and pepper. Remove from the heat and stir them through your mashed potato.

5 Tip your dough out on to a floured surface and roll out to your desired thickness. Shapes of knishes can vary, but a classic option is to use a pizza cutter to slice the dough into rectangles about the size of an envelope.

6 Place a spoonful of filling on the dough, paint the edges of the dough with egg wash, then fold the corners up and over the filling to form a parcel. Brush over with more egg wash and bake on a tray for 40 minutes.

TASTING NOTES

There's nothing subtle about a knish. Comprising mashed potato, sauerkraut, meat, onions, cheese and pastry, this is proper ballast, a carbohydrate hit of the very finest kind. It might be known as the 'humble knish', or 'lowly pie', but there's nothing cheap about its appeal. Bite through the hot, crisp pastry, and you hit thick, fluffy mashed potato, and, at its most basic, just onions – there are endless variations with a sharp hit of sauerkraut and meat, liver or beef. Dip the knish in mustard and eat it while it's hot. One is enough to keep the cold out. It shouldn't be bland; rather, it should be comfort food that warms the cockles of your heart. ● *by Tom Parker Bowles*

ORIGINS

Kuaytiaw is yet another Chinese contribution to Thailand's street food repertoire. Originally introduced by Chinese labourers, who popularised the dish during the early 20th century, today *kuaytiaw* is hands down the most common street food in Thailand. Versions involving spices and a curry-like broth were probably introduced via Muslim traders, while more recent spin-offs have resulted in a vast repertoire of entirely Thai varieties.

SERVES 1

THAILAND

KUAYTIAW

Kuaytiaw, or Thai noodle soup with pork or fishballs, is – dare we say it – the hamburger of Thai street food: it's simple, satisfying, cheap and ubiquitous.

YOU'LL NEED
300ml (10fl oz) pork or chicken stock
50g (1¾oz) fresh rice noodles or 40g (1½oz) dried rice stick noodles
5 small pork balls or 2 tbs cooked chicken, shredded
1 tsp white pepper, ground
a handful of beanshoots, trimmed
a handful of coriander leaves (cilantro), chopped
fried garlic or onion flakes
spring onions, chopped
red chillies, chopped
a wedge of lime, to garnish

METHOD
1 Boil the stock in a small saucepan.

2 Add the noodles, pork balls and white pepper and simmer for a few minutes until the noodles are cooked.

3 Pour the soup into a bowl and top with the beanshoots and coriander leaves.

4 Garnish with the fried garlic flakes, spring onions and as much chilli as you can handle. Squeeze over some lime juice. Serve immediately.

TASTING NOTES
Kuaytiaw is Thai comfort food, and doesn't pack the spicy punch of most of its counterparts. Yet despite its apparent simplicity, ordering *kuaytiaw* the Thai way requires a bit of knowledge, as diners are expected to specify what type of noodles they want, as well as their preference for meats or other toppings. Like other Thai noodle-based dishes, *kuaytiaw* comes out of the kitchen relatively bland and customers then season it with optional condiments including fish sauce, sugar, dried chilli flakes and vinegar. *Kuaytiaw* vendors span the most diverse spectrum of Thai street eats, and range from gritty streetside stalls to air-conditioned restaurants. Likewise, the dish functions equally well as breakfast, a late-night snack and anything in between. ● *by Austin Bush*

For the tomato sauce
3 tbs olive oil
½ cup onion, finely chopped
4 garlic cloves, chopped
400g (14oz) tomato puree
¾ tsp ground cinnamon
½ tsp ground cumin
½ tsp salt
¼ tsp ground black pepper
¼ tsp chilli flakes

For the kushari
1 cup long-grain rice
1 cup lentils (brown or black)
2 tbs white vinegar
½ tsp ground cumin
½ tsp garlic powder
8 tbs olive oil
1½ cups onion, sliced
1 cup pasta (small macaroni or
    vermicelli broken into small
    pieces)

ORIGINS

This cheap, filling and healthy national dish is so popular that some restaurants specialise in this alone, but little is known about its genesis. Educated conjecture suggests that it may have been created out of poverty or that, as vegan victuals, it was influenced by the vegetarian diet of fasting Coptic Christians. Whatever the case, meat – such as small pieces of fried liver, chicken or lamb – is now sometimes back in the bowl.

EGYPT

KUSHARI

SERVES 8

Opinions often diverge in Egypt, but one thing almost every Egyptian concedes is that *kushari* – a unique medley of pasta, rice and lentils with tomato sauce – reigns supreme.

METHOD

For the tomato sauce

1 Heat the oil and onions on a medium flame until the latter are golden brown.

2 Stir in the garlic and cook for two minutes.

3 Add the tomato puree, cinnamon, cumin, salt, pepper and chilli flakes. Increase the heat a bit and let simmer, uncovered, until the sauce thickens (approximately 15–20 minutes).

For the kushari

1 Simultaneously, but in different pots, cook the rice and the lentils. The lentils should simmer, covered, until tender (20–30 minutes); then, use a strainer to remove the lentils (leaving the lentil water in the pot), placing them directly into a mix of the vinegar, cumin and garlic powder.

2 Heat the oil on a medium flame; add the onions and cook, deglazing as necessary, until they are lightly browned. Remove from the oil and drain on paper towel.

3 Stir the uncooked pasta into the same oil used for cooking the onions; saute the pasta until it is lightly browned, then place it in the used lentil water, bring back to a boil and cook until tender.

4 Assemble the *kushari* in eight bowls: lay down a base of rice, add a blanket of pasta with a few browned onions, and then a cover of lentils. Spoon the tomato sauce on top and garnish with a few more onions.

TASTING NOTES

Kushari is a delectable, any-time-of-day, year-round whole that is more addictive than the sum of its humdrum parts: pasta, rice and lentils. The magic finish comes from a spicy tomato-sauce topping and garnish of fried onions, all enhanced by garlic-vinegar or chilli. It is assembled in a few seconds – but the experience is downright percussive. In *kushari*-specific restaurants, the cooked ingredients are doled out from a drum set of food-filled basins. As it happens, the *kushari* composer raps his spoon against the bowls and basins in a virtuosic display of rhythm. It's loud but mesmerising, a *Stomp*-style performance that begs an encore. Or is it just that the *kushari*'s so good one bowl is never enough?

● *by Ethan Gelber*

ORIGINS

During Hungary's cold winters, locals needed some serious sustenance to keep their bodies warm and fuelled; potato dough was the best choice around. This scrumptious snack was originally a by-product of bread-making in rural villages. Traditionally, the *lángos* was made from leftover dough and baked in a brick oven – its name derives from the local word for 'flame' – and would be served for breakfast on bread-baking days.

YOU'LL NEED

1 large potato, boiled, peeled and mashed
2½ tsp dried yeast powder
1 tsp sugar
1¾ cups plain (all-purpose) flour
1 tbs vegetable oil
¾ tsp salt
½ cup milk
2 cloves garlic, sliced in half
salt
dill, chopped, to taste

TASTING NOTES

The smell that emanates from this warm, doughy snack is heavenly, and after you've smeared it with juice from a cut garlic clove, you'll never be able to wolf down another run-of-the-mill pizza-dough fritter again – the *lángos* easily trumps it. Something of a *lángos* revival has spread throughout Hungary in recent years, with growing numbers of street vendors serving customers who are nostalgic for a filling food that tastes very Hungarian. Today, you'll often find *lángos* stalls cropping up wherever people are milling about: stations, beaches along Lake Balaton or the Danube, and fairs and markets. At any of these, you'll find that *lángos* happens to be excellent with creamy garlic soup – just don't plan on kissing anyone afterwards. ● *by Roger Norum & Strouchan Martins*

SERVES 1

HUNGARY

LÁNGOS

Deep-fried, frisbee-shaped bread puffs rubbed with a clove of garlic and topped with shredded gruyère or emmental cheese and sour cream, *lángos* (lahn-gosh) are a filling, quintessentially Hungarian afternoon snack.

METHOD

1 Place all ingredients – except the garlic, second measure of salt and the dill – in a mixing bowl. Mix the ingredients until moist.

2 Using an electric mixer with a dough hook, knead the mixture for approximately six minutes or until smooth. Place it in a greased bowl, cover and let it rise until its size has roughly doubled.

3 Separate the dough into four separate portions, then shape into rounds on a lightly floured board. Cover and let sit for 20 minutes.

4 In a large frying pan, heat the oil to 350°C (662°F). Flatten, then stretch the dough to discs roughly 20cm (8in) in diameter.

5 Fry individual dough pieces for about two minutes on each side or until golden brown. Absorb grease by placing cooked rounds on paper towel.

6 Rub the cooked *lángos* with the cut side of a garlic clove, sprinkle with salt and chopped dill, then serve.

TIP *Try adding toppings to your* lángos *– mushroom, cheese, beef, eggplant and cabbage are all common ingredients.*

INGRID HECZKO © GETTY IMAGES

YOU'LL NEED

4 x 450–500g (1lb) live lobsters

¼ cup mayonnaise

½ cup celery, diced

2 tbs unsalted butter, room temperature

4 hot-dog buns

4 leaves of Boston lettuce (or other crunchy, mild variety), washed

paprika or cayenne pepper (optional)

ORIGINS

Once so plentiful it was considered a poor-man's food, lobster got a makeover in the 1800s when New England society women realised they could enjoy the crustacean in salad form, rather than have to do the 'distasteful' work of cracking the shell themselves. In the early 1900s, someone came up with the idea of piling the lobster salad on a bun, and so the lobster roll was born.

SERVES 4

MAINE, USA

MAINE LOBSTER ROLL

A summer staple of the New England yacht-set, the lobster roll combines the haute (silky, sea-flavoured lobster meat) and the humble (mayonnaise, white-bread hot-dog buns) to drool-worthy effect.

METHOD

1 Put the lobsters in the freezer for a few hours (to 'numb' them before cooking).

2 Bring a large pot of water to a boil and cook the lobsters until they turn bright red (about 10 minutes). Plunge the lobsters into an ice bath to stop the cooking process.

3 Crack the lobsters and remove the tail and claw meat – check out the Gulf of Maine Research Institute's tutorial on eating lobster for tips on meat-removal techniques (www. gma.org/lobsters/eatingetc.html).

Pat the meat dry with paper towels, trim it into 1.5cm (3/5in) chunks, then refrigerate until cool.

4 In a large bowl, mix the meat with the mayonnaise and celery.

5 Butter the hot-dog buns and toast them under the broiler (grill) or in a pan until golden brown, then line them with a lettuce leaf and fill them with a quarter of the lobster-meat/ mayo mixture. Finish by sprinkling with paprika or cayenne pepper, if desired.

TASTING NOTES

A lobster roll is best enjoyed at a lobster shack in Maine. Some of these are beachfront, while others are found on the outskirts of historic fishing villages or perched atop pedestrian bridges. Wherever the location, a good shack will always have a line at lunchtime – don't be deterred! Order, then stake out a table as you wait for your number to be called. At last, claim your tray, where an overflowing lobster roll sits wedged inside a tiny paper basket. Depending on the shack, your first bite may be warm and buttery, or cool and mayo-slicked. Either way, it will be perfection: the silkiness of the meat, the softness of the bun, the crunch of lettuce... bliss. ● *by Emily Matchar*

ORIGINS

Mangue verte may have evolved from *buggai*, a spicy green mango chutney. It's served with *thieboudjenne*, the national lunch, and the communal bowl in which it's served is cordially fought over. It may also have travelled up from Guinea-Bissau or Senegal's Casamance region, famous for having the best mangoes. There, green-mango juice is made by sun-drying the unripe fruit for three days, then boiling it and adding sugar.

SERVES 1

SENEGAL

MANGUE VERTE

Mangue verte (green mango) has more in common with potato chips than yellow mangoes. On a hot day, it proves a refreshing combination of salty, crunchy and tart.

YOU'LL NEED

1 green mango
½ small lime (optional)
salt or a crushed Jumbo (a kind of MSG stock cube) or other stock cube
chilli powder

METHOD

1 Peel the mango, then slice it.

2 Squirt a bit of lime juice on to the fruit if you like it tangy, and toss.

3 Sprinkle over the crushed stock cube, salt and chilli to taste.

TASTING NOTES

Green-mango season coincides with Senegal's hottest period of year, so it is a time of bittersweet anticipation. It's sunny, the air is dry, and everyone is walking more slowly. Even the women who sell *mangues vertes*, their hair tied up in colourful scarves, prepare the snack at a sedate pace, slicing the mango of your choosing into a bag and shaking it up with the toppings. The mango is hard as an apple, and the first taste is salty and crunchy, followed by the bite of the chilli, but then the mango comes through, its sweetness just a glimmer and its sourness a fruity kick – a burst of energy on a hot day.

● *by Amy Karafin, with Maïmouna Ciss*

YOU'LL NEED

1 tsp active dry yeast
1¼ cups warm water
2½ cups white flour
1 tsp salt
1 tsp vegetable oil
optional toppings (such as
  cheese, yoghurt, herbs,
  sliced cooked lamb)

ORIGINS

In Lebanon, back in the day, women brought their dough to community ovens and baked large collective loaves. Then modern times brought commercially produced bread, and bakers shifted to single-serve, spice-mix-smeared breakfast helpings of *man'oushe bil-za'tar*. Today, *man'oushe* is a catch-all term describing the snack of bread adorned by any number of ingredients – *za'tar*, *jibneh* (cheese), *qawarma* (lamb) and more – for all tastes (sweet, savoury, herbivore, carnivore and omnivore).

LEBANON

MAN'OUSHE

Man'oushe is commonly (and unfairly) misprized as simply the Lebanese version of pizza. Instead, it is more like the crispy-crusted snack-emblem of the nation – affordable, all-purpose and classless.

METHOD

1 Dissolve the yeast in the warm water and set aside.

2 Sift two cups of flour and the salt together in a bowl and then slowly stir first the oil and then the yeast water into the flour.

3 Knead the dough for about 10 minutes until it is soft and stretchy. Roll it into a ball and set aside in a cloth-covered, flour-coated bowl for up to two hours, or until the ball has doubled in size.

4 Divide the dough ball into four equal parts and then punch each one down. Let rise for 30 more minutes.

5 Preheat the oven to 200°C (400°F).

6 Roll each of the four parts into a ball and coat with flour (shake off the excess). Then roll them out into 20–25cm (8–10in) discs about 4mm (⅛in) thick. They can be thinner and larger if you have a *saj*.

7 Add toppings (prepared separately).

8 Bake in the oven for 10–15 minutes or until the bottom of the bread is crisp and golden brown. Alternatively, cook on a hot saj for three to five minutes.

TASTING NOTES

Given the ubiquity of *man'oushe* in Lebanon and the huge diversity of trimmings, there is no quintessential eating experience associated with it other than the powerful sensory connection with Lebanon. The warm, baked-bread freshness of *man'oushe* and the unique seasoned zing of *za'tar* (an aromatic mix of wild thyme, sumac, sesame seeds, salt and oil) are, to most Lebanese, the strongest olfactory and gustatory triggers of their home when they travel abroad. This holds true whether they're from the bustle of Beirut's bohemian Hamra or the pastoral ease of the mountainous hinterland, and whether they prefer the thinner, slightly crispier and often larger disc cooked on the *saj* (an inverted wok) or its oven-baked coequal. ● *by Ethan Gelber*

YOU'LL NEED

1 tbs olive oil
1 onion, chopped
400g (14oz) minced (ground)
    beef
1 tbs cornflour
175ml (6fl oz) beef stock
1 tbs Worcestershire sauce
2 tbs tomato paste
1 tsp Vegemite
4 sheets shortcrust pastry (or
    make your own)
1 egg, beaten
tomato sauce

ORIGINS

Pies may not be uniquely
Australian, but nowhere has
embraced the concept with
such gusto. It's the nearest
there is to a national dish, and
in 1990 the Great Aussie Meat
Pie contest was inaugurated
to reward the country's finest
exponents. It was early British
settlers who brought the pie
to Australia. Their popularity
boomed, and streetside pie
carts (originally horse-drawn)
proliferated. Save for the horses,
little has changed.

AUSTRALIA

MEAT PIE

As Aussie as koalas, Kylie and the Harbour Bridge, the humble meat pie epitomises the no-nonsense nation's unfussy attitude: cook beef, put in pastry, serve hot.

METHOD

1 Preheat the oven to 220°C (425°F).

2 Fry the onion in the oil in a frying pan for about 10 minutes, until soft.

3 Add the beef; cook, stirring frequently, until the meat is browned.

4 Combine the cornflour and 1 tbs beef stock in a small bowl.

5 Add the remaining stock, Worcestershire sauce, tomato paste and Vegemite to the meat mixture in the frying pan; stir to combine.

6 Add the cornflour mix to the meat; stir.

7 Bring to boil, then simmer until thick. Remove from the heat and leave to cool.

8 Cut the pastry into eight circles, four slightly larger. Press the larger circles into pie tins; fill with the meat mixture.

9 Place the smaller circles over the meat; press the edges to seal. Brush the tops with beaten egg.

10 Bake for 20 minutes or until golden. Serve with tomato sauce.

TASTING NOTES

There are gourmet specimens on sale, handmade with posh ingredients such as garlic prawns. And there are many places to buy them: corner shops, pubs, late-night vans. But to appreciate the full Aussie-ness of the meat pie, there's only one place to go: the footy. You'll need to jostle with fans to purchase your pie, served hot and slightly soggy in its little paper bag. First things first: unsheathe the golden delicacy and douse with tomato sauce. Second: wolf down while cheering/jeering men in tight, short shorts. The taste sensations are simple: seasoned gravy, robust enough to act as internal glue; meat of not the highest calibre, but satisfying nonetheless; pastry wilted, but holding things together. No nonsense. Very Australian. ● *by Sarah Baxter*

YOU'LL NEED

50g (1¾oz) rice
1 tbs vegetable or canola oil
1 onion, finely diced
1 tsp ginger, crushed
1 tsp turmeric
2 tbs shrimp paste
2 red chillies, chopped
60g (2oz) banana stem, sliced thinly
2 stalks of lemongrass, sliced thinly
3 cups fish stock
50g (1¾oz) gram flour
500g (1lb) dried thin rice noodles
200g (7oz) firm white fish, such as haddock, pollack or sea bass, sliced
lime wedges, fried onions, extra chopped chillies and fresh coriander leaves (cilantro) to serve

ORIGINS

Mohinga is made from an almost exclusively indigenous repertoire of ingredients, suggesting that the dish has its origins in Myanmar. Some suspect that the noodles, which are made from rice by a complicated and time-consuming process that is thought to date back several centuries, are also indigenous to the region. This stands in contrast with most other Southeast Asian noodle dishes, which can usually be traced directly back to China.

SERVES 4

MYANMAR (BURMA)

MOHINGA

Cherished as Myanmar's national dish, *mohinga* is a comforting noodle soup that exemplifies the earthy flavours of the country's cuisine via a combination of lemongrass, shallots, turmeric and freshwater fish.

METHOD

1 To prepare the rice, toss it in a heated pan until the grains are browned and slightly burnt (but not stuck to the pan) and crush using a mortar and pestle or a spice grinder. (Alternatively, the amount of gram flour can be doubled in place of the toasted rice.)

2 Heat the oil in a saucepan and fry the onion, ginger, turmeric, shrimp paste, chillies, banana stem and lemongrass until the onion has softened.

3 Add the stock and whisk in the gram flour and toasted rice. Simmer for approximately 15 minutes until the soup has thickened.

4 Add the rice noodles and continue simmering until the noodles are cooked.

5 Add the fish and cook for a further five minutes.

6 Serve immediately with a wedge of lime and garnished with fried onions, chopped chillies and coriander leaves.

TIP *Banana stems look like fibrous white leeks and taste very similar to the fruit. If you're unable to find them in Asian grocery stores, try substituting water chestnuts.*

TASTING NOTES

Generally associated with central Myanmar and that region's predominantly Burmese ethnic group, *mohinga* is nonetheless sold in just about every town in Myanmar, typically from mobile vending carts and baskets or basic open-fronted restaurants. *Mohinga* vendors are most prevalent in the morning. Ordering the dish is a simple affair, as the only optional ingredient is *akyaw* (crispy fritters of lentils or battered and deep-fried vegetables). The thick broth has flakes of freshwater fish (typically snakehead fish), a yellow/orange hue due to the addition of turmeric, and a light herbal flavour, thanks to the use of lemongrass. A bowl is generally seasoned in advance, but dried chilli and limes are usually available to add a bit of spice and tartness. ● *by Austin Bush*

ORIGINS

Believed to have been invented in India in the Middle Ages, *murtabak* was brought to Southeast Asia by Tamil Muslim traders as early as the 10th century. Since arriving on the Malay peninsula, *murtabak* styles have adapted to reflect local tastes and ingredients – Chinese-style egg and green onion is a favourite in Singapore, while a side of spiced curry is common in Malaysia.

YOU'LL NEED

For the dough

3 cups white flour
1 tsp salt
1 tsp ghee
1 cup lukewarm water
½ cup vegetable oil

For the filling

2 tbs ghee, plus extra for greasing
1 onion, finely sliced
2 garlic cloves, crushed
½ tsp ginger, freshly grated
1 tsp turmeric powder
1 tsp garam masala
500g (1lb) minced (ground) lamb
2 eggs, beaten
salt and pepper
2 tbs coriander leaves (cilantro), finely chopped
1 bird's eye chilli, finely chopped

TASTING NOTES

Across Singapore and Malaysia, snacking is practically a national sport. And all sports must have their stadiums, right? In these countries, this means chaotic night markets and hawker centres (outdoor food courts), where vendors outdo each other to prove that their dishes are best. Imagine stumbling into a Singaporean hawker centre at 8am after a night on the town. 'Murtabak?' asks a man behind one of many counters, tilting his head at you. Sure, you nod, and the next thing you know, you're feasting on a warm golden pancake, stuffed with heavily spiced minced (ground) lamb and onion, the pastry flaky in your mouth. Wash it down with hot, sugar-laced tea, and you'll be fortified for another night of fun. ● *by Emily Matchar*

MAKES 6

MALAYSIA & SINGAPORE

MURTABAK

A stuffed pancake bursting with anything from lamb to egg to onions to peanuts, *murtabak* are a culinary symbol of the Muslim presence across Southeast Asia.

METHOD

1 Put the flour and salt in a large bowl and add the ghee, mixing with your hands.

2 Add the water and mix until a soft dough is formed, then knead on a floured surface for an additional 10 minutes.

3 Divide the dough into six equal-sized balls and put them in a bowl with the oil. Allow to sit for an hour.

4 Meanwhile, prepare the filling. Heat the ghee over medium heat and fry the onion until it's soft, about ten minutes.

5 Add the garlic and ginger and fry until the onion is golden brown. Add the turmeric and garam masala and stir.

6 Add the meat and cook, stirring constantly, until well browned.

7 Beat the eggs in a small bowl with the salt and pepper and set aside.

8 On a smooth oiled surface, take one of the dough balls and flatten it with a rolling pin. Press and stretch the dough with your fingers until it's so thin it's nearly translucent.

9 Heat a griddle or heavy pan on high and grease it with more ghee. Quickly transfer the dough to the griddle, using the rolling pin to drape the dough to aid the transfer.

10 Pour a small portion of beaten egg on to the dough and spread it around with a spoon to cover the centre.

11 Add one-sixth of the meat filling, then fold the dough over lengthwise.

12 When one side browns, flip the pancake, adding more ghee to the griddle if necessary.

13 Cook until golden brown and crisp on both sides.

ORIGINS

In the Bahasa Indonesia and Malay languages, the word 'otak' means brains. But don't let this keep you from trying *otak-otak*; the name comes from the colour and consistency of the dish, not its ingredients. Originating in Malaysia and Indonesia, *otak-otak* migrated to Singapore, where it quickly became a hawker-centre staple. Food-obsessed Singaporeans are said to cross the causeway into Muar in southern Malaysia for a taste of that town's *otak-otak* (said to be the region's best).

YOU'LL NEED

400g (14oz) deboned
   mackerel, minced
1 small onion, finely chopped
1 egg, lightly beaten
½ small turmeric leaf, thinly
   sliced
2 kaffir lime leaves, thinly
   sliced
2 tbs laksa leaves (Vietnamese
   mint), thinly sliced
1 tbs oil (optional)
½–¾ cup coconut cream
1 tbs sugar
salt, to taste
banana leaves, cut to
   20cm x 10cm (8in x 4in)
   and microwaved for 1 min
   to soften

For the spice paste

1.25cm (½in) turmeric root (or
   ¼ tsp powdered turmeric)
2–4 red chillies
4 pieces galangal, sliced
   (ginger can be substituted)
1 lemongrass stalk
3 candlenuts
2 garlic cloves
6 shallots
1 tsp *belacan* (shrimp paste),
   dry-roasted

SINGAPORE, MALAYSIA AND INDONESIA

OTAK-OTAK

A hand-held fish, egg and onion pâté that comes in its own natural (and biodegradable) package? For convenience, deliciousness and environmental friendliness, this spicy Southeast Asian treat takes first prize.

METHOD

1 Grind the spice paste ingredients to a fine paste.

2 Combine the spice paste with all the other ingredients (except the banana leaves) in a mixing bowl. Adjust to taste with salt and sugar.

3 Spoon 2 tbs of the mixture on to each banana leaf. Fold the leaf and secure it with a toothpick on both ends.

4 Grill or barbecue for about 10 minutes and serve.

TASTING NOTES

At first glance, the sight of long green leaves charring may lead the uninitiated into thinking that *otak-otak* is some sort of grilled tropical vegetable. But the charred green leaf is the packaging only – inside you'll find a gelatinous cake that's spicy and aromatic (with just a hint of the ocean). *Otak-otak* is best eaten at a streetside stall or inside a hawker centre, perhaps with a bottle of Tiger beer or an iced Milo. Though generally eaten as a side dish with other items (skewered chicken or grilled prawns make for a great combination), four or five *otak-otaks* should be enough to hold you over until your next meal.

This recipe comes to us from Ruqxana Vasanwala at Cookery Magic in Singapore (cookerymagic.com). ● *by Joshua Samuel Brown*

YOU'LL NEED

12–15 fresh oysters or 20 from
  a jar of refrigerated shucked
  oysters
4 eggs, beaten
pinch of salt
pinch of white pepper
1 cup rice flour
40g (1⅓oz) tapioca starch
150ml (5fl oz) water
25ml (¾ fl oz) peanut oil
2 garlic cloves, finely sliced
10ml (⅓fl oz) soy sauce
20ml (⅔fl oz) rice wine
4 spring onions, roughly
  chopped
2 tbs coriander leaves
  (cilantro), roughly chopped
chilli sambal (optional)

ORIGINS

Oyster cakes are also known
as oyster pancakes or oyster
omelettes. In China they may
be called *ah oh chian* (Fujian),
o'jian (Hong Kong) or *orh lua*
(Taiwan). The variations on
the name, as well as of the
ingredients and cooking method,
allude to the dish's peripatetic
evolution. It originated in the
Chinese provinces of Fujian and
Guangdong, where seafood is
king. From here, it has surfaced
in Taiwan, Hong Kong, Malaysia,
Singapore and the Philippines.

SERVES 1

HONG KONG, CHINA

OYSTER CAKE

These hand-span-sized, savoury-smelling, deep-fried omelettes are tweaked Asia-style with a gluttonous dozen or so fat oysters and a smattering of aromatic herbs, condiments and chilli.

METHOD

1 Rinse the oysters briefly in fresh water, then sit them in a colander to drain.

2 Hand-beat the eggs, salt and pepper in a bowl.

3 In a separate bowl, mix the rice flour, tapioca starch and water together and stir until it becomes a thin batter.

4 Heat a large pan until hot. Add a glug of peanut oil. When the oil is hot, pour in the batter, swirl it around the base of the pan and cook for about 15 seconds.

5 Pour in the egg mixture and leave until the bottom layer is cooked and the top layer is almost set.

6 With a wooden spoon, push the mixture to all sides of the pan, creating a small hole. Pour in the remaining oil and garlic, and saute.

7 Repeat with the oysters, soy sauce and rice wine until the oysters are warmed through and the mixture is set. Remove from the pan.

8 For night-market authenticity, cover with spring onion and coriander leaves, and serve with a big dob of chilli sambal or similar.

TASTING NOTES

Night markets are the ideal hunting ground for oyster cakes. Look for the stack of Chinese-style melamine plates wrapped in greaseproof paper. Behind them, there'll be a lady with a spatula in hand who will pour batter, spring onions and a ladle brimming with oysters into a bowl, before dunking it into the deep-fryer. Once cooked, the still-sizzling golden cake is doused in chilli sauce, sprinkled with market-fresh coriander and upended into a brown paper bag complete with wooden chopsticks. A yin-and-yang-esque equilibrium between crunch and flavour is paramount for the perfect oyster cake. The best have a thin outer layer of crunch, like a hash brown, and an inner eggy flavour. Coriander takes the edge off the fat. And chilli sauce? Well, that's the icing on the oyster cake. ● *by Penny Watson*

YOU'LL NEED

2 sesame-seed bread rolls,
  sliced lengthways
vegetable or canola oil, for
  deep-frying

For the panelle
  (chickpea fritters)
250g (9oz; about 1 cup) gram
  flour
1½ cups water
salt and pepper, to season

For the crocchè
  (potato croquettes)
500g (1lb) potatoes, peeled,
  boiled and mashed
1 tsp cornflour
handful of fresh parsley,
  chopped
salt and pepper, to season

ORIGINS

Panelle trace their origins back
to the Arabs who ruled Palermo
in the 10th century. While
chickpeas were already known
throughout the Mediterranean,
it was the Arabs who first
ground them into flour, and
who introduced sesame seeds
to Sicilian kitchens. Over time,
potato croquettes were added,
creating an affordable, carb-
intensive treat. Some *friggitorie*
(fry-shops) stamped patterns
on to the *panelle*; most popular
were fish designs, prized by the
poorest Palermitans as a low-
cost alternative to fried fish.

PALERMO, SICILY, ITALY

PANE, PANELLE E CROCCHÈ

The top draw at Palermo's outdoor food stalls is this unusual, North African–influenced sandwich stuffed with herby chickpea fritters and crunchy potato croquettes.

METHOD

1 To make the chickpea fritters, combine the gram flour and water in a saucepan over medium heat. Season well with salt and pepper.

2 Bring to the boil while continuously stirring to remove any lumps, until the mixture becomes thick like a paste.

3 Remove from the heat. Using a wooden spoon, take dollops of the mixture and spread it thinly – about 0.5cm (¼in) thick – on the surface of a round plate.

4 When the mixture has cooled on the plate, slice into eight even triangular sections (like a pizza) using a butter knife.

5 Fry the fritters in a deep-fryer or heavy-bottomed saucepan.

6 To make the potato croquettes, mix the mashed potatoes with the cornflour and parsley and season well with salt and pepper.

7 Take a golf ball-sized amount of the mixture and shape into croquettes.

8 Fry the croquettes in a deep-fryer or heavy-bottomed pan, until golden and crisp.

9 To assemble the sandwich, put a few slices of the chickpea fritters and two or three potato croquettes in the bread roll and serve immediately.

TASTING NOTES

Step into Palermo's streets on a sunny morning and you'll be greeted by a cacophony of vendors singing out the virtues of their produce. Follow their voices into Palermo's tangle of back-alley markets, navigating past mounds of artichokes, strawberries, tomatoes and eggplants, through stalls piled with olives, sausages and cheeses. Eventually you'll reach the street carts where *panelle* are sold, their presence announced by the crackle of oil and the stacks of golden fritters emerging from the fryer. Best when crisp and hot, these delights are soul-satisfyingly soft and tooth-pleasingly crunchy, their flavours punctuated with hints of sesame from the all-enclosing roll. To complete the experience, shake on a little salt, squeeze on some lemon juice, and bite in! ● *by Gregor Clark*

ORIGINS

Food historians have found mentions of *pastizzi* by merchants prior to the 16th century, when Malta's fabled Knights Hospitaller fortified the capital of Valletta. More than that may never be known, however, as the local cuisine is a heady mix of many cultural influences and the once-resident Phoenician, Greek, Carthaginian, Roman, Byzantine, Ottoman, Arab, Italian and British populations.

MALTA

PASTIZZI

Pastizzi are savoury, diamond-shaped pastry puffs stuffed with creamy cheese or spicy peas, often (inaccurately) called 'cheesecakes' in English. Diminutive, divine and most delectable when steaming hot, they're quintessentially Malta.

YOU'LL NEED

300g (11oz) ricotta cheese
2 eggs
handful of parsley, finely
    chopped
750g (1½lb) puff pastry
1 egg
salt and pepper, to taste

METHOD

1 Combine the ricotta, eggs, parsley, and season. Mix thoroughly.

2 Roll out the puff pastry so that it is quite thin. Measure and cut out circles that are approximately 9cm (3½in) in diameter.

3 Beat the egg and brush along the edges of each circle. Drop a dollop of the filling on to the centre of each and then fold it in half, sealing along the joined edge.

4 Coat with egg wash and then bake in a medium-hot oven for 30 minutes or until the pastry is golden brown.

TASTING NOTES

The Maltese discuss and eat *pastizzi* the same way young newlyweds cavort in public on their wedding night: with tender devotion thinly disguising animal ravenousness. No matter what time of day it is, whether you're on the street, in a nondescript *pastizzeriji* at 5am or at home with friends, eating *pastizzi* is serious business. Hot treat in hand, everyone pauses to absorb the initial sensory wave of buttery, cheesy, spicy delight. The first bite detonates the crust, spraying pastry crumbs over everything, followed swiftly by the hot, intoxicating surge of filling. For both first-timers and aficionados, it's visceral. The proof is that there's always room for just one more. ● *by Ethan Gelber*

ORIGINS

Since the US embargo took effect in the 1960s, Cuba had been relying on the Soviets for trade but, following the Fall of the Wall, Russia pulled the plug on this arrangement and financially woeful times ensued... Necessity being the mother of invention, delights like grapefruit-rind steak and pizza for a peso cropped up, using basics and leftovers to fill bellies.

YOU'LL NEED

1 x 30cm (12in) thin-crust pizza base (either store-bought or homemade)
mustard
tomato paste, unseasoned
Swiss cheese and American muenster cheese, to taste (1:3 ratio)
dill pickles, sliced
leftover roast or slow-cooked pork, shredded
adobo seasoning

MAKES 1 PIZZA

CUBA

PESO PIZZA

A faithful streetside hunger-buster since the economic sanctions of the post-Soviet era, peso pizza is testimony to Cuba's turbulent past and a refreshing change from the touristy restaurants.

METHOD

1 Preheat the oven to 230°C (450°F).

2 Spread some mustard over the pizza base, then add a liberal amount of unseasoned tomato paste.

3 Grate the desired amount of cheese and mix together. Sprinkle half the grated cheese mixture over the base. Authentic peso pizza should have more cheese than tomato, so the tanginess of the cheese comes through.

4 Add the dill pickles and some pre-cooked shredded pork, then top with the remaining cheese.

5 Sprinkle with *adobo* seasoning and bake for 6–8 minutes or until the crust is golden brown. Fold in half to serve.

TASTING NOTES

Why the long queue outside such a humble-looking booth? Queuing is a Cuban specialty right up there with cigars, so the wait might be the longest prequel to buying street food you'll ever have. But when the other options are an ice-cream man, a bland restaurant or a poorly stocked local shop, peso pizza is a winner. The crust is thin and crunchy. The toppings are an assortment of tomatoes and a pungent, slightly bitter-tasting Swiss-style cheese with additions of pickles, mustard and, on very good days, pork offcuts or salami. And it's Cuba's most enjoyable snack. This is mainly because you eat peso pizza like calzone, folded over with the ingredients hitting you all at once. ● *by Luke Waterson*

ORIGINS

Phat kaphrao is a relatively recent introduction to Thai cuisine and didn't become commonplace until about 50 years ago, although holy basil has long been a Thai staple. In ancient India, the herb was used in ayurveda and is considered a sacred plant among Hindus. Because *phat kaphrao* is fried in a wok, the dish – like much Thai street cuisine – most likely has at least partial Chinese origins.

TASTING NOTES

Unlike other street dishes in Thailand, there generally aren't any vendors who specialise only in *phat kaphrao*. Rather, the dish is typically sought out at *raan ahaan taam sang* (made-to-order) carts, stalls and restaurants. These establishments do a huge variety of dishes and are recognised by a tray or case of raw ingredients. A diner will have a look at what is available and place his or her order directly with the cook. The steaming dish emerges from the wok a few minutes later. Although *phat kaphrao* is predominately salty and spicy, it is always served with a bowl of sliced chillies in fish sauce and sometimes a squeeze of lime – the Thai equivalent of the salt shaker. ● *by Austin Bush*

SERVES 4

THAILAND

PHAT KAPHRAO

While *phat kaphrao* might not have the same sort of instant name recognition as, say, *phat thai*, this spicy, meaty stir-fry is actually the go-to one-dish meal for many Thais.

YOU'LL NEED

¼ cup plus 2 tbs fish sauce
6 bird's eye chillies, chopped
1 tbs lime juice
1 tbs coriander leaves
  (cilantro), chopped
5 tbs peanut (groundnut) or
  vegetable oil
4 garlic cloves, peeled and
  coarsely chopped
400g (14oz) minced (ground)
  pork, preferably a coarse
  consistency
1 tsp white sugar
½ cup water
3 large handfuls of holy basil
  leaves
steamed rice, to serve
4 fried eggs, to serve

METHOD

1 Make the fish sauce seasoning by mixing the ¼ cup fish sauce with four of the chillies, the lime juice and coriander leaves. Set aside.

2 Heat the oil in a wok over medium heat.

3 Fry the garlic and the rest of the chillies but do not let the garlic go brown.

4 Add the pork mince and stir-fry until nearly cooked. Season with the remaining fish sauce and the sugar.

5 Add the water and simmer for a few minutes until some of the water has evaporated.

6 Remove the wok from the heat and stir in the basil.

7 Serve on a bed of steamed rice, topped with the fish sauce seasoning and a fried egg.

TIP *This dish is traditionally very spicy so use the number of chillies as a guide and feel free to add as many more as you can handle. Beef or chicken may be substituted for the pork.*

ORIGINS

Phat thai, which allegedly dates back to the 1930s, is a relatively recent introduction to the Thai kitchen and, despite the nationalistic name, is in many ways more of a Chinese than a Thai dish. Both noodles and the technique of frying are Chinese in origin, although the dish was invented in Thailand and its seasonings are characteristically Thai. Today, it is quite possibly Thailand's most beloved culinary export and remains a popular one-dish meal in Bangkok and central Thailand.

YOU'LL NEED

4 tbs tamarind concentrate
6 tbs palm sugar
2 tbs fish sauce
5 tbs peanut (groundnut) or vegetable oil
8 red shallots, coarsely chopped
3 duck eggs
300g (11oz) fresh rice noodles; or 250g (9oz) dried rice noodles, blanched in boiling water
60g (2oz) firm tofu, cut into cubes
2 tbs dried prawns, rinsed and dried
1 tsp salted radish, rinsed, dried and finely chopped
2 tbs roasted peanuts, coarsely chopped
2 handfuls of beanshoots, trimmed
1 handful of Chinese chives, sliced into 2cm (1in) lengths
extra beanshoots and roasted peanuts, fresh chillies and lime wedges, to serve

SERVES 4

THAILAND

PHAT THAI

Phat thai is the most famous Thai dish in the world, and understandably so: you can't go wrong with gooey strands of noodles, crunchy peanuts, tart lime and singed egg.

METHOD

1 Mix the tamarind concentrate with the palm sugar and fish sauce until the sugar dissolves. Set aside.

2 Heat the oil in a wok over medium heat.

3 Fry the shallots until they begin to colour.

4 Crack in the eggs and stir them until they resemble scrambled eggs.

5 Turn up the heat and add the noodles. Add the tamarind mixture and let simmer for a few minutes.

6 Stir in the tofu, dried prawns, radish and peanuts and continue stirring until most of the sauce is absorbed.

7 Add the beanshoots and chives and stir for a few minutes.

8 Transfer to a bowl, top with more beanshoots and roasted peanuts and serve immediately with fresh chillies and lime wedges on the side.

TIP *Have all the ingredients prepared and ready to go next to your wok as the dish takes very little time to cook. The duck eggs may be substituted with chicken eggs, and the red shallots with French shallots or brown onions but the rest of the ingredients are key to the dish's salty, sweet and sour taste, and should be readily available from Asian supermarkets.*

TASTING NOTES

Although nowadays *phat thai* is sold in restaurants, it's still an important part of the streetfood repertoire. Stalls selling the noodles also tend to serve *hoy thot*, a mussel omelette. Both are generally fried on the same flat, round surface, but some vendors choose to fry *phat thai* in a wok. *Phat thai* is among the milder Thai street dishes and diners are expected to boost the flavour with a personalised mixture of fish sauce, sugar, dried chilli and ground peanuts. Served with sides that possess a slightly bitter taste, including banana flower and garlic chives, true *phat thai* is a largely vegetarian dish containing only dried shrimp and fish sauce, although modern versions sometimes include fresh shrimp or prawns.

● *by Austin Bush*

ORIGINS

Pho has its origins in the cuisines of France and China and was popularised around the end of the 19th century. The Vietnamese took the rice noodles from their northern neighbour and a taste for red meat from the colonialists, and created something new. Some say *pho* (pronounced 'feu') is derived from the French dish *pot au feu*, while others argue that it is Chinese in origin, stemming from a Cantonese word for noodles, *fan*.

YOU'LL NEED

For the broth

10cm (4in) piece of ginger
2 yellow onions
cooking oil
2.25kg (5lb) beef marrow or oxtail bones
4.75l (5 quarts) of water
1 cinnamon stick
1 tsp coriander seeds
1 tbs fennel seeds
5 star anise
2 cardamom pods
6 whole garlic cloves
¼ cup fish sauce
2 tbs sugar
1 tbs salt

For the noodles & garnishes

225g (½lb) beef steak
450g (1lb) dried flat rice noodles
10 sprigs mint
10 sprigs coriander leaves (cilantro)
10 sprigs Thai basil
12 sawtooth coriander leaves
½ yellow onion, thinly sliced
2 limes, each cut into 6 thin wedges
2–3 chilli peppers, sliced
450g (1lb) beanshoots
hoisin sauce
hot chilli sauce

TASTING NOTES

Dawn is breaking across Vietnam and the hum of scooter engines has yet to reach its mid-morning crescendo. The *pho* sellers have set up stalls, some little more than a battered collection of metal pans, while others include plastic tables and gleaming trolleys. Whatever you choose, it's the broth that matters. This is the heart and soul of *pho* and should be rich and deeply flavoured, hinting at star anise, cardamom and coriander. The noodles should be freshly made, while the chillies are mild, rather than fierce. Beanshoots add a satisfyingly crunchy texture. A dash of fish sauce, a squeeze of lime, and breakfast is ready. Grab a wobbly chair, sit back and slurp. ● *by Tom Parker Bowles*

SERVES 8

VIETNAM

PHO

The breakfast of champions, this fragrant spiced Vietnamese noodle soup topped with slices of beef, brisket, chicken or meatballs and a squeeze of lime is the perfect wake-up call.

METHOD

For the broth

1 Halve the ginger and onions lengthwise and place on a baking sheet. Brush with cooking oil and put on the highest rack under a heated grill (broiler). Grill on high until they begin to char. Turn over to char the other side for a total of 10–15 minutes.

2 Boil enough water in a large pot to cover the beef bones and continue to boil on high for five minutes. Drain, rinse the bones and rinse out the pot. Refill the pot with the bones and the 4.75L of cool water. Bring to the boil then lower to a simmer. Remove any scum that rises to the top.

3 Place the cinnamon stick, coriander seeds, fennel seeds, star anise, cardamom pods and garlic cloves in a mesh bag (alternatively, *pho* spice packets are available at speciality Asian food markets) and add to the broth pot along with the charred onion and ginger and the fish sauce, sugar and salt and simmer for 1½ hours.

4 Discard the spice pack and the onion and continue to simmer for another 1½ hours.

5 Strain the broth and return it to the pot. Adjust salt, fish sauce and sugar to taste.

For the noodles & garnishes

1 Slice the beef as thinly as possible across the grain.

2 Cook your noodles according to the packet.

3 Bring the broth back to the boil.

4 Arrange all the other garnishes next to your serving bowls.

5 To serve, fill each bowl with noodles and raw meat slices. Ladle the boiling broth into the bowls – this will cook the beef slices.

6 Garnish with the remaining herbs, onion, lime wedges, chillies, beanshoots and sauces, and serve immediately.

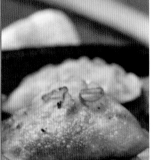

ORIGINS

Variations of stuffed dumplings can be found all over Europe and Asia, but the exact origin of *pierogi* remains unknown. A Dominican monk named Jacek, better known as the patron saint of *pierogi*, is generally credited for their popularisation by distributing them to the poor. This, in addition to their ease of preparation, has cemented their reputation as peasant food.

YOU'LL NEED

For the dough
4 cups plain (all-purpose) flour
1 tsp salt
1 egg
2 tbs olive oil
1 cup warm water

For the filling
2 large potatoes for mashing
120g (4oz) twarog cheese (or substitute with quark cheese)
1 medium onion, finely diced and lightly fried in olive oil

To serve
olive oil, for frying
sour cream, to garnish

TASTING NOTES

Don't be fooled by the appearance of *pierogi* as a seemingly bland pocket of dough. The best ones are soft and pillowy, and they come in infinite varieties. No Polish family gathering is complete without the classic potato and cheese, but equally popular is cabbage and sauerkraut. While wandering Poland's historical market squares, the moreish meat or *kielbasa* (a garlicky Polish sausage) *pierogi* will provide all the sustenance you need for the day ahead. In summer, treat yourself to blueberry or strawberry pierogi, served with lashings of cream.

The recipe given here is for *pierogi* with potato, cheese and onion stuffing. ● *By Johanna Uy*

MAKES ENOUGH FOR 6

POLAND

PIEROGI

Tasty, cheap and satisfying, these crescent-shaped doughy delights are a Polish icon found everywhere from church fundraisers to restaurants, with the variety of fillings limited only by the imagination.

METHOD

1 Peel the potatoes and add them to a pot of boiling water. Cook until soft.

2 While the potatoes are boiling, prepare the dough. Sift the flour and salt on to a flat surface and then, with your hands, mix in the egg, oil and half the water.

3 Knead the mixture for approximately 10 minutes, adding the rest of the water a little at a time (you may not need all of it), until you end up with a soft, elastic dough. Wrap the dough in plastic or cover with a damp cloth so it does not dry out while you prepare the filling.

4 Drain the potatoes and push them through a sieve or a potato ricer (aerating rather than mashing them will result in a fluffier filling). Combine the potato with the cheese and half of the fried onion. Season well and set aside.

5 Unwrap the dough and roll it out flat on your workspace to about 3mm (⅛in) thickness. Use a glass tumbler or cup to cut out circular shapes.

6 Put a teaspoon of filling in the centre of each circle. Fold the circle in half into a semicircle and seal the ends by pinching them together with your fingers.

7 To cook, place the *pierogi* in a pot of simmering (not boiling) water. Once they rise to the surface a few minutes later, remove them from the pot.

8 To serve, lightly brown the boiled *pierogi* for a few minutes in olive oil, then garnish with sour cream and the remainder of fried onions.

TIP *Any leftovers can be frozen after simmering, then thawed and lightly fried in a little oil when ready to eat.*

NICO DE PASQUALE PHOTOGRAPHY © GETTY IMAGES; RICHARD I'ANSON © LONELY PLANET IMAGES

YOU'LL NEED

30g (1oz) yeast
2 cups warm water
7 cups plain (all-purpose) flour
1½ tsp salt
2 tbs olive oil, plus extra to oil
    baking trays
toppings of your choice –
    tomato sauce, mozzarella,
    fresh basil, anchovies,
    olives...

ORIGINS

All pizza evolved from
unleavened flatbreads, and the
Persians and Greeks both claim
credit. But it's the Italians who
mastered the art. Although
the ingredients are simple,
pizza perfection is elusive. To
succeed, you need a white-hot
wood-burning oven and the
best ingredients you can afford.
The Roman version has a much
thinner crust, and, historically,
it was a flat bread. You'll find all
sorts now, but crisp and thin is
still king.

ROME, ITALY

PIZZA AL TAGLIO

Baked in giant metal trays, sliced in thick rectangular slabs and paid for by weight, flat-edged Roman pizza is perfect picnic food for fun on the run.

METHOD

1 Dissolve the yeast in one cup of the water, then combine all the dough ingredients and mix gently until a dough forms.

2 Knead the dough, either by hand or using an electric mixer with a dough hook, until you have an elastic texture and satin finish.

3 Transfer the dough to an oiled bowl, cover it and leave it in a warm spot until it doubles in size.

4 Lightly grease your baking trays and preheat your oven to 220°C (425°F).

5 On a floured surface, divide the dough into four portions, and roll out each one to fit your trays, trimming as needed.

6 Drizzle a little olive oil over the rolled-out bases, then start creating your signature pizza, using whatever toppings take your fancy. Just a couple of simple ingredients will do.

7 Bake for roughly 15 minutes or until the crusts are pleasingly golden. Cut into neat rectangles to serve.

TASTING NOTES

Good pizza, whether *al taglio* or Neapolitan (with a risen edge), is all about the crust. Any fool can slather on some tomato sauce and scatter over a few toppings, but only the masters can create a crust that renders all conversation useless. Avoid any place with a spongy crust. You want to find somewhere with queues of uncooked pizza and expectant crowds waiting for the oven to disgorge its treasure. Point at what you want and indicate how much. The cooks will then cut, weigh and hand it over to be eaten like a sandwich. The crust is brittle, the toppings spread with a generous hand. Don't worry about manners – scoff it down before it cools. ● *by Tom Parker Bowles*

ORIGINS

Seafood has probably always been eaten raw in Polynesia, particularly by fisherman who often spent several days at sea and had no choice in the matter. The Japanese introduced the idea of *sashimi* (eaten in French Polynesia as a heap of thinly sliced raw tuna on a bed of rice) in the last century while European and Chinese cultures brought their own vegetables and spices to the islands during early contact.

TASTING NOTES

Sweet from the coconut, tart from the lemon, savoury from the fish, *poisson cru* is as refreshing as a tickle of trade wind. It's usually prepared by Polynesian hands and ladled into plastic takeaway dishes alongside a heaping portion of steamed rice. It's eaten for dinner at a *roulotte* (mobile food van), among families sharing the dish alongside *steak frites* (steak and chips) and chow mein, the night sticky with smoke from open-air grills. The rice soaks up the coconut flavour of the sauce and softens the crunch of the vegetables; the raw tuna takes on the texture of a firm *mousse torte*, tender and silky. The scent of flowers adds the final touch to gustatory paradise. ● *by Celeste Brash*

SERVES 4–6

POISSON CRU

If flower-scented air and turquoise lagoons could be blended into a dish, *poisson cru* would be it: raw fish and vegetable salad dressed with lime juice and coconut milk.

YOU'LL NEED

500g (about 1lb) fresh yellowfin tuna, cut into 2.5cm (1in) cubes (salmon, swordfish, bonito and other deepwater fish can also be used)

¾ cup fresh lime or lemon juice (or a mix of both – they shouldn't be too sour)

2 tomatoes, chopped

½ small onion, finely chopped

1 cucumber, finely chopped

1 carrot, grated

1 green pepper, thinly sliced (optional)

1 cup coconut milk

spring onion or parsley, chopped (optional)

salt and pepper, to taste

METHOD

1 Take the tuna chunks and soak in a bowl of seawater or lightly salted fresh water (locals swear this makes the fish more tender) while preparing the vegetables.

2 Remove the tuna from the salt water and place in a large salad bowl. Add the lemon or lime juice and leave the fish to marinate for about three minutes.

3 Pour off about half to two-thirds of the juice (depending on how tart you like it), then add the vegetables and toss together with the fish.

4 Pour the coconut milk over the salad and add salt and pepper to taste.

5 Garnish with chopped spring onion or parsley and serve with white rice.

YOU'LL NEED

For the chicken gravy
2 cups chicken stock
1 tbs butter
2 tbs flour

For the fries
5 potatoes, peeled and sliced
 into fries
vegetable oil, for frying
400g (14oz) fresh cheese
 curds

ORIGINS

According to legend, in
1957 someone walked into
a restaurant in Warwick,
northeast of Montreal, and
asked the owner, Fernand
Lachance, to toss some cheese
curds in with his potatoes.
Lachance complied but said,
*'Ça va faire une maudite
poutine!'*. ('That's going to
make a damn mess!') Jean-Paul
Roy, a restaurateur in nearby
Drummondville, claimed that he
invented the complete poutine
a few years later when he added
gravy to the mix.

QUEBEC, CANADA

POUTINE

**It may be a 'damn mess', but it's a damn delicious mess.
It's the Quebecois creation called *poutine*: potatoes
swimming in gravy and sprinkled with cheese.**

METHOD

1 Prepare the gravy. If using a ready-mixed sauce, simply warm according to the packet instructions.

2 If making your own gravy, melt the butter in a saucepan and stir in the flour until it becomes a yellow paste.

3 Slowly whisk in the stock, ensuring it is free of lumps.

4 Let it simmer for approximately 10 minutes until the volume reduces by about a third. Remove the sauce from the heat and set aside.

5 While the gravy is simmering, rinse the potatoes in cold water and dry thoroughly.

6 Deep-fry or shallow-fry the potatoes until golden brown.

7 Place the fries in a shallow bowl and top with the cheese curds and smother with the gravy. Serve immediately.

TIP *A classic* poutine *is usually made from St Hubert packet sauce and fresh cheese curds, which are readily available in Quebecois supermarkets. Shredded mozzarella and ready-mix chicken gravy are acceptable substitutes.*

TASTING NOTES

Stab your fork into the pile of potatoes and pull out a starchy spear, drenched in gravy and dripping with cheese. It's not elegant, but it's a perfect cure for the munchies after a last call at the pub. It's a staple of ski resorts, casual eateries and chip stands, too – fast-food stalls sell burgers, hot dogs and sometimes fried fish along with *poutine*. Wherever you're indulging, let your *poutine* sit for a minute or two, so the cheese begins to melt and soak into the gravy. Don't wait too long or the potatoes will get soggy. You want the ideal balance of crisp potato, soft cheese and gooey gravy. ● *by Carolyn B. Heller*

ORIGINS

Pupusas were already being cooked up almost 2000 years ago. Archaeologists have found cooking equipment used to make *pupusas* in Joya de Ceren, often described as El Salvador's Pompeii. Until the middle of the 20th century, they were a speciality of the central regions alone. But as the population became mobile in the 1960s, they spread across the country and to neighbouring states too.

YOU'LL NEED

For the pupusas

2 cups *masa harina* (maize flour)
1 cup warm water
assorted fillings: for a cheese filling, grate a combination of your favourite cheeses (try mozzarella or Swiss) and add a hit of minced green chilli; for a quick pork version, you can blend cooked bacon with a zingy tomato sauce; or you can even used leftover potatoes pepped up with jalapeños – invent your own!

For the curtido

½ green cabbage, shredded
1 carrot, grated
4 cups boiling water
½ cup water
½ cup cider vinegar
½ tsp salt
1 jalapeño or serrano chilli, minced
3 spring onions, minced

TASTING NOTES

El Salvador is not exactly feted for its native food, but a decent *pupusa* is a world-class bite. There's barely a street, from main thoroughfare to winding dirt track, where you won't find a *pupuseria*. And it's adored by peasant and politician alike. Make sure yours is cooked fresh before your eyes – not so much for reasons of hygiene, but pure, visceral pleasure; they taste so much better fresh off the hot plate. Cheap, rich and filling, the quality is generally high, while the *curtido* (usually available in mild or spicy) cuts a vinegary swathe through all the stodge. Go for a mix of cheese, beans and pork for the ultimate hit, all washed down with local Suprema beer. ● *by Tom Parker Bowles*

EL SALVADOR

PUPUSA

Often described as the national dish of El Salvador, these fat, stuffed tortillas available on every street corner fulfil your every dietary need: bread, meat, cheese and vegetables.

METHOD

For the pupusas

1 Mix the *masa harina* with the water to form a malleable dough that is firm but not dry. Add water in small increments if needed. Cover and leave to rest for five to ten minutes.

2 Divide the dough into even portions and roll each piece into a ball. Make a deep indentation into the dough with your thumb – big enough to accommodate a small spoonful of filling. Pinch the dough closed over the filling, then gently flatten the ball into a disc in the palm of your hand.

3 Place a disc between two pieces of wax paper and carefully roll it out with a rolling pin until it's about 6mm (¼in) thick.

4 Place an oiled skillet (frying pan) over a medium to high heat and cook *pupusas* for one to two minutes on each side, until they are browned and a little crispy. Serve with the *curtido* and salsa.

For the curtido

1 Place the cabbage and carrots in a large bowl. Pour over the boiling water to cover the vegetables and set aside for about five minutes. Then drain in a colander, pressing out the liquid.

2 Return the cabbage mixture to the bowl and toss with the remaining ingredients. Cover and chill for a couple of hours (or preferably overnight) to lightly ferment.

YOU'LL NEED

1½ cups dried black-eyed peas

salt

3 ripe but slightly firm plantains

½ cup palm oil, plus a little extra for taste

salt

2 small onions, finely sliced

minced fresh chilli

2 garlic cloves, sliced (optional)

2 ripe tomatoes, diced

3 cups vegetable oil

shito, to taste (omit if vegetarian)

1 tbs *gari*

ORIGINS

Everyone loves red red, but it's a favourite of the Ewe ethnic group and may have migrated from Ewe country in eastern Ghana (the Volta Region) and Togo. There, as in Accra, beans are an inexpensive protein, which makes red red Ghana's national cheap lunch. Over time, *gari* (fermented, dried cassava powder) was added for texture and, since it expands with water, as a cheap stomach-filler; *shito* (shee-to; peppery fish sauce with spices) was added for heat.

GHANA

RED RED

The only thing better than Ghanaian dishes may be their names. Hot, sweet and spicy, red red pairs beans with fried plantains and *zomi* (red palm oil).

METHOD

1 Rinse the peas and then let them soak for an hour minimum.

2 Drain the peas and rinse them again.

3 Cook the peas in a saucepan with three cups of water. Bring to boil for a minute or two then reduce the heat and let simmer until soft (about 45 minutes).

4 When they are cooked, drain, toss in a couple of pinches of salt, and set aside.

5 Chop the plantains in four, cutting at a diagonal so the slices make a wedge-like 'spoon'. Dribble water over them and sprinkle over salt to 'cure' them (it increases their sweetness). Let them sit for a few minutes.

6 In another saucepan, heat ½ cup of palm oil. Add the onions and chilli (garlic optional) to the oil once hot; stir until crispy. Add the tomatoes and stew until soft.

7 Heat up some vegetable oil in a third pan and add the plantains, a few at a time, stirring to ensure even frying (a couple of minutes will usually do it). Remove when golden brown.

8 Add the palm oil, onion and chilli mixture to the finished peas. Dribble some more zomi and some shito on top and then sprinkle gari over it. Serve with fried plantains. Red red is eaten with the right hand: use the plantain to pick up the peas.

TASTING NOTES

Red red's natural habitat is 'chop bars' (shacks serving lunch) and roadside stands. If you wait near others who are already eating, you'll hear, 'You are invited!' – the traditional polite offering to share food. The scene is crowded with people lunching, while a woman with a basket of pineapples on her head passes by, ready to cut up one for dessert. The red red is hot and the oil on the plantains still sizzling when it is served. The beans are soft and salty and the plantains are soft and sweet with crispy edges – the tastes are meant to go together. The *gari* gives it an extra crunch, the palm oil gives it depth and the *shito* gives it a kick.

● *By Amy Karafin, with Gladys Noi*

SERVES 8 AS A SNACK

EUROPE

ROASTED CHESTNUTS

No other aroma evokes the spirit of winter and festivities more vividly than roasted chestnuts. One whiff of their sweet and earthy smell will have you humming that Christmas tune...

YOU'LL NEED

500g (1lb) chestnuts

METHOD

1 Preheat the oven to 200°C (400°F).

2 With a small, sharp knife, carefully score a cross or a slit on each chestnut. Place the chestnuts in a shallow roasting tray with slit sides facing up.

3 Roast until the skins break open and the nuts are soft, approximately 30 minutes.

4 Serve in paper cones with mugs of mulled wine.

TIP *Scoring the chestnuts is critical to prevent them from exploding in the oven. Of course, chestnuts can also be roasted over an open fire. A street vendors' secret is to boil the chestnuts first for about 15 to 20 minutes before grilling and giving them that 'roasted' look.*

TASTING NOTES

Few can resist the waft of roasting chestnuts from a street cart on a chilly day. Snacking on a bag of hot chestnuts roasted over an open fire, or on open coals as they do in Padua, is the quintessential European holiday-season experience. The unpleasantness of raw chestnuts is miraculously transformed, with their sweet taste and fuller flavour emerging only after a good toasting. In Rome, street vendors go the extra mile and arrange individual chestnuts about to burst in their split shells in neat gold-and-brown rows. As nuts go, chestnuts are literally tough ones to crack. Peeling them while still warm is part of the ritual and your efforts will be rewarded with their delicate, nutty taste and rich texture. ● *by Johanna Uy*

YOU'LL NEED

For the chapati
3 cups white flour
6 tbs vegetable oil
50ml warm water
salt, to taste

For the omelette
8 eggs
2 handfuls shredded cabbage
2 handfuls tomato, thinly cut
optional additional fillings:
    onion, pepper, avocado,
    chopped
salt and pepper, for seasoning

ORIGINS

The word rolex comes from 'rolled eggs' – as in eggs rolled in chapati. Essentially the same as the egg roll you get in India (though arguably fresher and tastier in Uganda) – the rolex has its origins in Uganda's eastern city of Jinja. Home to a sizeable Indian community, locals catered to their tastes by cooking cheap and filling chapati snacks. Ubiquitous these days across Uganda, Jinja is still considered to have the country's best rolex offerings.

UGANDA

ROLEX

Cherished for its simplicity and fresh flavours, Uganda's rolex
(rolled chapati filled with tomato-and-cabbage omelette) has
gained mythical status among travellers. Whether a late-night feed
or lunch-time pitstop, this tasty roadside snack always hits the spot.

METHOD

For the chapatis

1 Mix the flour with salt and two tablespoons of oil and slowly add half of the warm water, kneading until you get a dough consistency.

2 Divide the mixture into four balls, and roll each into a thin circle on a lightly floured surface.

3 Add half a tablespoon of oil to a frying pan on a medium heat, and cook each side of the chapati for several minutes until dark brown patches appear. Brush more oil on either side and cook until firm and floppy. Set aside, and repeat the process.

For the omelette

1 Break two of the eggs into a cup and whisk with a fork, before adding a quarter of the chopped tomato and cabbage and a pinch of salt.

2 Pour the mixture into a frying pan on a high heat. After several minutes, flip the mixture. Lay one chapati directly on top of the omelette, and cook for a few minutes before flipping the two together again.

3 Remove the chapati and omelette from the heat together, with the latter on top. Add more slices of fresh tomato, and other fresh ingredients (if using), and a pinch of salt and pepper. Roll into a tube shape. For maximum authenticity, serve in a clear plastic bag to prevent drippage.

4 Repeat process until all four rolex are rolled and ready to eat.

TASTING NOTES

From Kampala's chaotic streets to dusty rural towns, across Uganda you'll find vendors cooking up rolex. Watching it being prepared in front of you is part of the fun. Set up along busy intersections, bus stations and markets, rolex carts are equipped with sun umbrellas, glass casing topped with a crate of fresh eggs and a rounded charcoal-fuelled brazier. The eggs are whisked together with chopped tomato and cabbage in a colourful plastic cup before being tossed dramatically upon the sizzling hotplate. With a chapati placed on top, it's then flipped and prodded, before being expertly rolled and served steaming hot in a plastic lunch bag to be wolfed down. Delicious! Costing less than 50c, it's fast food, Ugandan-style. ● *by Trent Holden*

ORIGINS

Traditionally eaten by Iraqi Jews on Saturday morning, *sabih* – known as *bid babinjan* (egg in eggplant) back in its native Baghdad – was brought to Israel by Iraqi immigrants in the early 1950s. For years appreciated mainly in Tel Aviv suburbs with large populations of Iraqi Jews, the delectable dish has recently created a buzz among Israel's young and trendy set, especially in ultra-hip Tel Aviv.

YOU'LL NEED

4 eggs
lots of onion peels
1–2 young *baladi* (Levantine heirloom) eggplants, cut into slices 2–3cm (¾–1¼in) wide and 75mm (⅓in) thick
1–4 potatoes, depending on size, peeled and diced into 1cm (⅓in) cubes
salt and finely ground pepper
tahini paste
1 garlic clove
1 tsp lemon juice
2–4 fresh tomatoes, chopped into pencil-eraser-sized cubes
4 Mediterranean (Persian) cucumbers, chopped into pencil-eraser-sized cubes
1 onion, peeled and finely diced
mildly hot green chilli peppers, very finely chopped
vegetable oil
4 fresh pita
amba
handful of parsley, chopped

TASTING NOTES

Ask an Israeli of Iraqi origin where to find the best *sabih* and chances are you'll hear about long-ago Sabbath mornings in Baghdad. Traditionalists swear by the old-time recipes, on offer in hole-in-the-wall shops, while modish *feinshmekerim* ('connoisseurs' in Israeli slang and Yiddish) often champion sleek eateries. But what everyone is looking for is the perfect mixture of flavours and textures. As you bite through the still-warm pita the ingredients take centre stage for cameo roles and then merge into the background harmonies: warm eggplant meets parsley; juicy tomato nuzzles up to soft morsels of egg; tangy *amba* mixes with crisp onion; and the heat of chilli is mellowed by creamy tahini. ● *by Daniel Robinson*

YADID LEVY © GETTY IMAGES

ISRAEL

SERVES 4

 SABIH

Felafel's little brother combines fried eggplant and hard-boiled egg with tahini, *amba* (Iraqi-style mango chutney) and chopped veggies to create a cheap, filling and healthy meal in a pita pocket.

METHOD

1 Add the eggs and onion peels to a large pot of cold water, bring to a boil and then let simmer for several hours until the whites of the eggs have turned light brown. (Another way to achieve this effect is to simmer the eggs in black tea).

2 Place the eggplant strips in a single layer on a strainer, add salt and let it sit for an hour. Rinse and pat dry.

3 Boil the potatoes with a pinch of salt. Drain, sprinkle with salt and pepper and set aside.

4 Place 3 or 4 tsp of tahini paste in a small bowl and add enough water to create a thick liquid. Crush the garlic clove into a paste and add to the tahini along with the lemon juice and some salt and pepper. Stir thoroughly.

5 Mix together the tomato, cucumber, onion and chilli.

6 Deep-fry the eggplant slices in vegetable oil for seven or eight minutes.

7 Take a pita bread and make a horizontal slit near one edge. Spread some tahini inside and add a smear of *amba*.

8 Place slices of eggplant and potato along one wall of the pita. Top with chopped parsley and tomato-and-cucumber salad and season with salt and pepper.

9 Crush a peeled brown egg with a spatula (yes, just mush it) and place it on the wall of the pita opposite the eggplant and potato.

10 Add salt, pepper, chopped parsley and a dollop of tahini to the top of the pita. Press the pocket together so it will fit in your mouth.

IDRIS AHMED © GETTY IMAGES

YOU'LL NEED

For the filling
225g (½lb) diced beef
1 cup chopped onions
1 tbs chopped garlic
¼ cup cubed mutton fat
1 tsp cumin
1 tsp salt
1 tsp pepper

For the dough
2½ cups plain (all-purpose) flour
1 egg
½ cup warm water
2½ tbs margarine, melted

ORIGINS

The *samsa* (or *somsa*) originated in the ancient city-states of Samarkand, Bukhara and Khiva, located in modern-day Uzbekistan. It was a popular street snack among merchants and Silk Road travellers, who stocked up on the meat pies before a long journey. Abul-Fazl Bayhaqi (AD995–1077), a Persian historian, mentioned the *samsa* in his work *Tarikh-e Mas'oudi* (Masoudian History). *Samsas* eventually made their way to the Kashgar, Yarkand and Hotan as well as India, where it evolved into the samosa.

MAKES ENOUGH FOR 3 SERVINGS

CENTRAL ASIA

SAMSAS

This lightly spiced mutton-filled pastry has been a perennial favourite among the hungry caravan men, spice merchants and travellers along the Silk Road throughout the centuries.

METHOD

1 In a mixing bowl, combine the diced beef, chopped onions, garlic and cubed mutton fat. Add the cumin, salt and pepper. Mix well and refrigerate for 45 minutes.

2 Prepare the dough by combining the flour, egg and water. Knead the dough until it attains a thick consistency, but don't overwork it. Roll it into a tube shape and then slice it into sections, each a little bigger than a golf ball.

3 Preheat the oven to 200°C (400°F).

4 Sprinkle some flour on your work surface and roll out the ball-shaped pieces of dough into a rectangle with a rolling pin. Lightly brush the dough (on both sides) with melted margarine.

5 Using a spoon, add a dollop of the meat mixture to the centre of the dough. Fold the edges of the pastry over the meat mixture in either a triangular or rectangular shape. Press the corners and edges together to prevent leakage. Repeat.

6 Place the *samsas* on a greased baking sheet, seam side up. Bake for 25 minutes until the tops are golden brown.

TASTING NOTES

Deep in every bazaar of central Asia stands the venerable *samsa* chef, his black smock streaked with ash and a white cap covering his head. At the crucial moment, he scoops up his golden-brown bounty using a large iron ladle on a wooden pole. The smell of mutton fat rises and mingles with the other scents of the market. Hungry patrons purchase *samsa* by the plateful and huddle over small tables, a hair's breadth away from the chaos of the bazaar. The first bite is dangerously hot, but once your palate becomes acclimatised to the heat, you'll appreciate the juicy mutton, savoury onion, aromatic spices and crisp, buttery envelope that combine to create a true taste of Central Asia. ● *by Michael Kohn*

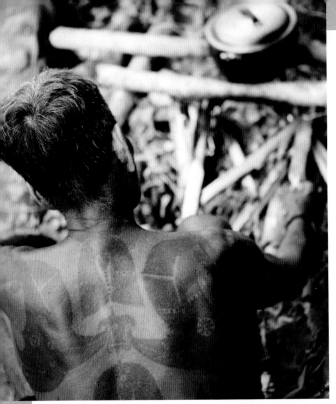

YOU'LL NEED

8 cups water
Sarawak *laksa* paste
8 prawns
2–3 cups chicken stock
½ cup coconut milk
2–3 eggs
butter, for frying
2 handfuls *bee hoon* noodles
1 handful beanshoots
100g (¼lb) shredded chicken
   breast
coriander leaves (cilantro), to
   garnish
1 lime
sambal belacan

ORIGINS

Most purveyors of Sarawak *laksa*
are, like *bee hoon* noodles,
of Chinese origin, but in the
finest Malaysian tradition this
dish brings together a variety
of culinary influences, including
classic Nyonya (Peranakan)
ingredients like *sambal belacan*.
Sarawak *laksa* shares little more
than its name with the *laksa*
dishes of Peninsular (West)
Malaysia and Singapore, such as
asam laksa (fish and tamarind
soup) and curry *laksa* (a fusion
of curry and coconut milk).

SARAWAK, MALAYSIA

SARAWAK LAKSA

SERVES 2

Tangy, spicy, oh-so slurpable and lip-smackingly good, Sarawak *laksa* is a supremely satisfying way to begin the day. It's the dish Sarawakians most often crave when they're away from Borneo.

METHOD

1 In a pot, bring the water to the boil then add Sarawak *laksa* paste. Stir every few minutes for 30 to 45 minutes.

2 In a separate pot, boil the prawns in chicken stock until cooked, then remove and slice lengthwise.

3 Add the chicken stock to the Sarawak *laksa* pot. Simmer over a low heat for a few minutes.

4 Pour the liquid into a third pot through a fine-mesh strainer to remove any solid particles. Continue to simmer.

5 Add coconut milk to taste. Stir the broth every few minutes.

6 Beat the eggs, the fry in a little butter to produce a very thin omelette; slice into strips.

7 Soak the *bee hoon* noodles in hot water until soft and then place in boiling water for three minutes. Transfer the noodles to two medium-sized bowls.

8 Add beanshoots, shredded chicken breast, halved prawns and omelette strips to the bowls.

9 Ladle just enough broth into the bowls to cover the noodles.

10 Garnish with chopped coriander leaves and squeeze the juice of half a lime into each bowl.

11 Add *sambal belacan* to taste.

TASTING NOTES

You're in Kuching and it's 7.30am, so following a tip you stroll to a cafe famous for its Sarawak *laksa*. Inside, men and women – mostly Chinese, but also Malay and Dayak – read newspapers or chat in a babel of dialects as they dig into oversize bowls with chopsticks and spoons. Inside each one, a tangle of vermicelli noodles, swimming in oil-flecked broth, is topped with crunchy beanshoots, orange-white shrimp, strips of omelette, chicken bits and vibrant coriander leaves. Occasionally, someone adds a dollop of fiery *sambal belacan* or a squeeze of calamansi lime. The air is redolent with the tang of chilli, galangal and lemongrass and the heady aromas of coriander and coconut milk. ● *by Daniel Robinson*

ORIGINS

YOU'LL NEED

For the dough
1 cup warm milk
1 tsp dried yeast powder
1½ cups plain (all-purpose) flour
1 tbs olive oil
1½ tbs sugar
½ tsp salt

For the filling
⅓ cup pine nuts
500g (1lb) minced lamb
1 large onion, finely diced
1 large tomato, chopped
1 handful fresh mint or coriander leaves (cilantro), finely chopped

2 tsp salt
1 tsp allspice
¼ tsp cinnamon
¼ tsp cayenne pepper
2 tbs natural yoghurt
1 tbs tahini
1 tbs pomegranate molasses
2 tbs butter

wedges of lemon and natural yoghurt, to serve

TIP
It's fine to use basic pizza dough for the crust. Pomegranate molasses or thickened sauce can be found at Middle Eastern or Turkish supermarkets.

TASTING NOTES
On a sun-drenched Baalbek day, there's no better way to street feast after clambering over the Roman ruins. Luckily, the *sfiha* bakeries are only a stone's throw from the tumbled columns themselves. Pull up a chair and order up your plate. The tiny parcels arrive with their filling bubbling and the corners pinched in to keep it from oozing out. Drench with lemon and add a dollop of yoghurt before tucking in. They're quick to eat – two mouthfuls at the most – but with the satisfying savouriness of summer's myriad flavours. The mint-kissed lamb has a tahini twist topped off by piquant pomegranate. When only crumbs remain, it's the toasted crunch of pine nuts that you're left to relish. ● *by Jessica Lee*

SFIHA

These bite-sized morsels, which combine the best bits of pizza and pie, have a sweet-and-sour pomegranate punch that sums up the taste of Lebanon in one mouthful.

METHOD

1 In a bowl, combine the milk and yeast. Set aside in a warm place for five minutes, until it begins to froth.

2 Sift the flour into a separate bowl and stir in the olive oil, sugar and salt. Stir in the frothing milk mixture. Cover the bowl with a cloth and set aside for five minutes.

3 Knead the dough for around 10 minutes on a lightly floured surface, until it becomes smooth and elastic. Cover with a cloth, place in a warm place and allow it to rise for one to two hours, until it has doubled in size.

4 Once the dough is ready, prepare the filling. First, lightly toast the pine nuts in a frying pan.

5 In a large bowl, combine the meat, onion, tomatoes, mint, salt and spices. Add the yoghurt, tahini, pomegranate molasses, toasted pine nuts and butter and mix well.

6 Divide your dough into walnut-sized balls by rolling them between your palms.

7 Place the dough balls on a floured surface and use a rolling pin to flatten each ball into a circle, about 8cm (3in) in diameter.

8 Place 1 tbs of the meat filling in the middle of each circle, flattening the mixture into a cube-like shape.

9 Lift the edges of each circle up to encase the filling by pinching the corners together.

10 Brush an oven tray lightly with olive oil and place the pastries on it.

11 Bake at 180°C (350°F) for 30 minutes or until the pastry is golden and the filling sizzling.

12 Serve with wedges of lemon and dollops of natural yoghurt.

YOU'LL NEED

4 tbs palm sugar
3 tbs fish sauce
2 tbs tamarind concentrate
4 tbs lime juice
4 garlic cloves
salt
4 bird's eye chillies
3 tbs roasted peanuts
3 tbs dried prawns, rinsed and
dried
8 cherry tomatoes, quartered
4 snake beans, chopped
3 cups green papaya,
shredded

ORIGINS

Som tam most likely has its origins in neighbouring Laos, where it's known as *tam maak hung* and is a culinary staple. Residents of northeast Thailand, who have many cultural and culinary links with Laos, probably introduced the dish to the rest of Thailand during their stints as migrant labourers as early as the 1950s. It didn't take long to catch on, and *som tam* can now be found in virtually every corner of the country.

THAILAND

Spicy, tart, crunchy, salty and sweet – five reasons why *som tam*, an often ballistically-spicy green papaya 'salad' that combines them all, is quite possibly Thailand's best loved street-food dish.

METHOD

1 Make the dressing by mixing the palm sugar, fish sauce, tamarind concentrate and 3 tbs of the lime juice.

2 Using a large mortar and pestle, crush the garlic with some salt, then add the bird's eye chillies, roasted peanuts, dried prawns and the rest of the lime juice and pound until it resembles a coarse paste.

3 Add the cherry tomatoes and snake beans and lightly bruise (but do not crush) with the paste.

4 Put the green papaya in a large salad bowl, stir in the paste and the dressing and gently toss with a large spoon.

5 Serve as a side dish in a Thai banquet or with steamed rice and raw vegetables such as cabbage and green beans.

TIP *Try to make this salad a couple of hours before serving so that the papaya can absorb all the flavours.*

TASTING NOTES

Although now served in some restaurants, *som tam* is still associated with the street stalls run by residents of northeast Thailand. As is often the case with Thai-style street food, ordering *som tam* requires advance discussion, with diners telling the woman operating the mortar and pestle how many chillies or how much sugar they prefer. Thais from northeastern Thailand tend to prefer 'Lao'-style *som tam*, which contains *plaa raa* (unpasteurized fermented fish sauce) and chunks of eggplant. Most others go for 'Thai' *som tam*, which is sweeter, containing peanuts and dried shrimp and seasoned with bottled fish sauce. Either way, the application of chilli and lime juice provide the defining flavours of *som tam*: spicy and tart. ● *by Austin Bush*

ORIGINS

These date right back to the Eastern Jin dynasty (AD317–420), when people would cook up thin flour cakes and eat them with vegetables to celebrate the beginning of spring. Then, they were known as 'spring cakes'. Later on, in the Ming and Qing dynasties, there was a custom of 'biting spring' – eating the cakes to welcome in the new season. In time the 'spring cake' evolved into the spring roll.

YOU'LL NEED

For the filling

2 cups beanshoots
6 dried shiitake mushrooms
2½ tbs oyster sauce
1 tbs chicken broth (water is an adequate substitute)
2 tsp light soy sauce
1 tsp sugar
2 tbs oil, for stir-frying
55g (2oz) canned bamboo shoots, finely sliced
½ red pepper, diced
1 medium carrot, grated
salt and pepper, to taste

For the rolls

18–20 spring roll wrappers
1 egg, lightly beaten
4–5 cups oil, for deep-frying
plum sauce or sweet-and-sour sauce, for dipping

TASTING NOTES

Crisp and fresh – that's the secret to the greatest spring rolls. You want the flour-and-water pastry to be golden and brittle, and the filling to leap around the mouth in great joyous bounds. This contrast lies at the heart of the spring roll's appeal. On the street, make sure they're cooked before you. They sit in neat rows, pale and soft, ready for the bubbling cauldron. A dash of vinegar is the perfect foil to the spring roll, and you'll find this, together with soy sauce, served alongside. They're eaten at all times of the day, as a cheap snack or part of a full meal. ● *by Tom Parker Bowles*

CHINA

SPRING ROLL

The ubiquitous spring roll is a crisp, paper-thin pastry wrapped arounda dazzling array of fillings, from carrots and beanshoots to shrimp, pork and duck. Bite, crunch, grin.

METHOD

For the filling

1 Rinse and drain the beanshoots. Soak the dried mushrooms in warm water. Let the beanshoots dry and the mushrooms soak for 30 minutes.

2 Squeeze the excess water out of the mushrooms, then slice them thinly.

3 Mix the oyster sauce, broth, soy sauce and sugar into a small bowl. Set aside.

4 Spread 2 tbs hot oil around a frying pan. Once sizzling, add the dried mushrooms, then the bamboo shoots, followed by the red pepper, beanshoots and grated carrot.

5 Stir in the oyster-sauce mixture and add salt and pepper to taste.

For the rolls

1 Lay one wrapper with a corner towards you, then paint the edges with egg.

2 Place 2 tbs of the filling across the bottom half, not quite to the edges. Fold the bottom corner of the wrapper over and tuck it under the filling, fold in the left and right sides, then roll. Brush the top corner lightly with egg, fold over and seal.

3 Place the roll seam-side down on a baking sheet and brush lightly all over with oil. Repeat with the remaining wrappers and filling.

4 Heat the oil for deep-frying to hot, then add several spring rolls at a time and cook until crispy and golden brown (approximately three to four minutes). Remove, then drain on a paper towel. (Healthy alternative: instead of frying, bake the rolls for 12–15 minutes at 180°C (360°F) until golden and crisp.)

5 Serve with plum sauce or sweet-and-sour sauce for dipping.

YOU'LL NEED

2 blocks of fresh, extra-firm
 tofu
2 jars *kimchi* (pickled
 cabbage, available from
 Korean supermarkets)
vegetable oil, for deep-frying
hot sauce, to serve

ORIGINS

It's likely that this dish migrated
to the island along with settlers
from China's southeast coast
during the early days of Han
Chinese settlement in the
17th century. It's possible
that stinky tofu's inventor was
someone in a predicament
similar to the first person to
eat *nattō* (a sticky, odorous
Japanese dish consisting of
fermented soybeans); namely,
a resourceful hungry person
looking for a way to make a
spoiled soy product palatable
and accidentally discovering
how to make it delicious.

TAIWAN

STINKY TOFU

Of the dishes available in night markets around Taiwan, the one that separates casual tourists from hard-core foodies is a local favourite – fermented bean curd (aka stinky tofu).

METHOD

1 Cut the tofu into 5cm (2in) cubes and place in a bowl with the liquid from both jars of *kimchi*. A shallow bowl works well, as the liquid should cover the tofu. You can also layer the *kimchi* itself between the tofu for an extra kick.

2 Cover the bowl with an airtight cover and set aside on a counter or, if the weather is warm, outside (warmth promotes fermentation). After about 48 hours you should notice some fermentation occurring – the liquid should be slightly fizzy, and there may be a mild (though not unpleasant) smell coming from the bowl. The longer you let it sit, the more pungent the tofu.

3 When you're ready to cook the tofu, heat up enough oil so that your cubes will be fully (or almost) covered.

4 Squeeze any additional liquid from your cubes and fry until they're golden brown.

5 Drain and serve with *kimchi* and hot sauce. Whereas street-vendor stinky tofu (with its long fermentation time) has a flavour similar to a ripe camembert, yours might taste more like a mild brie – not a bad place to start for the uninitiated!

TIP *Stinky tofu is not a dish most folks make at home. For one thing, to make it requires a fermentation process lasting weeks or even months. For another thing, it stinks. This recipe produces a reasonable (though less odiferous) version that gives a genuine approximation of the night-market variety.*

TASTING NOTES

Taiwan's night markets are filled with strange sights, sounds and smells, and perhaps the strangest of all is stinky tofu. You'll likely smell it before you see it – it's sold from a stand consisting of a deep fryer, dripping rack and little else. Your nose might suggest that someone's left some cheese out in the sun or is maybe deep-frying unwashed socks. But fear not, for as any Taiwanese will tell you, 'Stinky tofu smells bad, but it tastes good.' Give in to culinary adventure and try some; you'll discover it's crispy on the outside and soft within, with a flavour akin to ripe camembert. Stay in Taiwan long enough and you may even develop a taste for it. ● *by Joshua Samuel Brown*

ORIGINS

Pigs, chickens, cows, goats, sheep and coriander were all introduced to the Americas by early Spanish invaders. But the taco is the only true pre-Hispanic dish that remains untouched and unchanged, adored by the Olmec, Maya and Aztec civilisations alike. *Tacos al pastor* is a Mexico City classic and a dish with Middle Eastern roots. Brought to the city by Lebanese emigrants in the 1950s, it's a doner kebab made from pork rather than lamb.

MAKES 16 TACOS

MEXICO

TACOS

If maize is the heart of Mexican food, then the ubiquitous taco, a soft corn tortilla stuffed with all manner of delectable ingredients, is its soul.

YOU'LL NEED

500g (1lb) minced (ground) beef
garlic salt, to taste
16 corn tortillas
olive oil, for frying
3 serrano chillies, chopped (you can substitute jalapeños)
1 medium onion, finely sliced
1 tomato, diced
1 bunch coriander leaves (cilantro), chopped
2 avocados, sliced
2 limes, cut into wedges
salt, to taste

METHOD

1 In a frying pan, cook the ground beef with a couple of dashes of garlic salt until browned. Drain off any fat and set aside.

2 Take your tortillas and lightly brush them with olive oil. Put a large frying pan on a high heat and lightly fry the tortillas so they are still soft but have got a bit of colour on them.

3 Remove from the heat and let them drain on paper towels.

4 Now to assemble the tacos. Place a spoonful of meat on each one, then add the chillies, onion, tomato, coriander leaves and avocado. Squeeze a wedge of lime across it, sprinkle with salt, roll it up and serve. You can also add grated cheese, shredded lettuce, salsa – whatever you like.

TASTING NOTES

If it's a good taco stall, there'll be a queue. As the scent of cooking meat and warm tortillas mingles with cigarette smoke and diesel fumes, your appetite will be honed to an unbearable edge. Don't worry if the stall is little more than a bicycle with a propane heater, or a rundown pushcart. It's the food, not aesthetics, you're after. Four tacos make a civilised start, and you can always come back for more. Extra lime, salt and hot sauce will always be close by, so you can personalise and pique the palate. The taco might seem simple, but that contrast between soft tortilla and crisp pork is sublime. If food here is religion, then the taco is God. ● *by Tom Parker Bowles*

ORIGINS

There are records from the 17th century of a thin crepe popular in Tokyo and Osaka, which evolved into *okonomiyaki*, a thick egg pancake weighed down with toppings, and *choboyaki*, small batter balls. But it is Endo Tomekichi, a *choboyaki* vendor in Osaka, who is seen as the creator of *takoyaki*. He began, in the mid-1930s, to add octopus and other flavourings to his *choboyaki*. Now, it's one of the great foods of Osaka, and found across the country.

YOU'LL NEED

For the batter

1 large egg
1⅓ cups water
1⅓ cups cake flour, or 1 cup plain (all-purpose) flour and ⅓ cup cornflour
1½ tsp baking powder
½ tsp salt
1½ tsp sugar
1½ tsp instant *dashi* powder

For the filling

250g (½lb) boiled octopus, or substitute 3 large cooked shrimp, cut into small, thumb-sized cubes
2 tbs pickled ginger, finely chopped and squeezed to remove moisture
2 tbs spring onions, finely chopped
2 tbs green cabbage, finely chopped
1–2 tbs canola oil

To garnish

3 tbs mayonnaise (optional)
3 tbs Worcestershire sauce
1½ tbs *aonori*
½ cup *katsuobushi*

TAKOYAKI

MAKES ABOUT 16 DUMPLINGS

Takoyaki **are hot, crisp golf balls of octopus-spiked batter, bought from street vendors and slathered with sauce, mayonnaise and shaved bonito flakes, or carefully dipped into a sharp** *ponzu* **sauce.**

METHOD

1 First, make the batter. Whisk together the egg and water. Combine the flour, baking powder, salt, sugar and *dashi* in a bowl.

2 Make a well in the dry ingredients, then whisk in the egg mixture until smooth. Transfer to a measuring cup. Set aside for 15 minutes.

3 Heat a *takoyaki* pan over medium heat. Brush oil into each well.

4 Once the pan is just sizzling, pour the batter into the pan to just shy of the rim.

5 Add one or two pieces of octopus or shrimp and ample pinches of ginger, spring onion and cabbage to each well.

6 Wait one minute until the edges have begun to set and/or small bubbles have formed at the rim. Use skewers to loosen each dumpling at the top edge and flip it over.

7 Continue turning and rotating the dumplings until they attain a uniform light brown colour and are crisp (usually about five minutes). Move the dumplings to a plate using a skewer or tongs. Oil and repeat the cooking to make more dumplings.

8 Splash the mayonnaise and Worcestershire sauce on top of each dumpling, followed by the *aonori* and the *katsuobushi*. Serve hot.

TIP *These scrumptious dumplings are meant to be eaten hot straight out of the pan – the lightly crisp morsels lose their crispness in under a minute. If you don't have a* takoyaki *pan, then a Pancake Puff pan or* ableskiver *pan (for Danish pancakes) works well.*

TASTING NOTES

It's the smell that grabs you first: a hint of onion, a whisper of cephalopod, a sweet fug as a ladle of batter is poured into tiny moulds. Chunks of tentacle are dropped in each, covered by spring onions and *tenkasu* (little crunches of tempura batter). Then the real art begins. With pointed steel chopsticks, the cook deftly pokes and turns each ball, creating a perfect golden sphere. Once done, they're packed into a polystyrene box and anointed with mayonnaise, a coating of *takoyaki* sauce and a layer of shaved bonito. Grab your cocktail stick and dig in. The shell is firm and chewy, bursting open to reveal a not-quite-set mass of batter, the octopus chunk the final treat. ● *by Tom Parker Bowles*

ORIGINS

Found all over Central and South America, tamales are an ancient food that pre-dated the arrival of Europeans by millennia. There's evidence of their existence as far back as 8000BC; they were a staple for Aztecs, Mayans, Olmec, Toltecan and even Inca civilisations. Today, chicken or pork filling with salsa or *mole* (a thick, complex sauce) are the most popular, along with poblano chillies and cheese.

YOU'LL NEED

For the filling

500g (1lb) pork loin
1 large onion, halved
1 garlic clove
4 dried California chilli pods (similar to poblano chillies)
2 cups water
1½ tsp salt

For the dough

500g (1lb) dried corn husks
⅔ cup lard (can use vegetable shortening)
300ml (10fl oz) beef stock
2 cups *masa harina* (maize flour)
1 tsp baking powder
½ tsp salt
1 cup sour cream

TASTING NOTES

Look for vast steel containers (*tamaleras*) leaking steam, which loiter on almost every street corner. This is a snack for even the most cautious of gastronauts, as all those hours of steaming make for a particularly safe mouthful. This is glorious super stodge and you'll struggle to eat more than two. The wrapper is not edible and is to be discarded once finished. The fillings are mere bit parts when compared to the main event, the steamed dough itself. It should sing of maize, with the sort of texture that softly and subtly succumbs to the onslaught of teeth. *Atole*, a thick porridge-like drink sweetened with coarse sugar, cinnamon and vanilla, is usually sold alongside. ● *by Tom Parker Bowles*

MAKES ABOUT 16 TAMALES

MEXICO

TAMALE

Breakfast bliss or twilight snack, these steamed, corn-husk-clad masa delights are comfort food, Mexican-style. Filled with anything from pork to pineapple, this is hand-held ballast of the finest kind.

METHOD

1 Put the pork, onion and garlic in a large cooking pot and cover with water. Bring it to the boil, then reduce to a simmer until the meat is tender (about two hours).

2 Deseed the chillies (use rubber gloves to avoid transfer-burn!) and simmer them in a pot of two cups of water for 20 minutes. Remove from the heat.

3 When it has cooled, blitz the chillies and water in a blender until smooth. Strain, add the salt and set aside.

4 When the pork is done, shred it with two forks and stir in one cup of the chilli sauce.

5 Soak the corn husks in warm water.

6 With an electric mixer, beat the lard (or shortening) with a tablespoon of beef stock until it whips up and becomes airy.

7 Stir the *masa harina*, baking powder and salt together in a separate bowl and gradually add to the shortening mix, adding more broth as needed until you have a dough with a bouncy texture.

8 Drain the corn husks and pat dry. Spread the dough over the husks (no thicker than 6mm or ¼in), put a spoonful of the pork in the middle and fold the sides of the husk inwards like you're packaging up a parcel. Place in a steamer and cook for an hour.

9 When they're done, peel away the husks, pour over a little of the chilli sauce and top with a knob of sour cream.

ORIGINS

Hard-boiled eggs date back to antiquity, but tea eggs are a distinctly Asian twist on a classic dish. It's likely that the tea egg's distinctive flavouring and cooking method developed as a way to keep the dish palatable longer in the days prior to refrigeration. Tea, of course, is traditionally Chinese, though nowadays tea is but one of the dish's spicing agents, with star anise, soy sauce and other spices being the more dominant flavours.

SERVES 6

TAIWAN & CHINA

TEA EGGS

**This tasty snack food is found throughout Taiwan.
A tea egg crock pot is as ubiquitous in a Taiwanese convenience
store as a hot dog roller grill in an American 7-11.**

YOU'LL NEED

6 large eggs
2 tbs loose black tea, or 2
teabags
¼ cup dark soy sauce
1–2 whole star anise

METHOD

1 Hard-boil the eggs. Remove from the heat and allow to cool for handling.

2 Tap the eggs all over with the back of a spoon so the shells crack (do not peel – the cracking allows the flavour to seep in).

3 Place the eggs in a pot, ideally one large enough for all six eggs to fit on the bottom. Cover with the tea leaves, soy sauce and star anise, and enough water to cover the eggs fully.

4 Bring to the boil, then simmer on a low heat (a crock pot works nicely), with the pot uncovered, for 90 minutes, adding water as needed.

5 Your resulting tea eggs, when peeled, should have a nice marbled look, with egg whites being tan with darker streaks of brown. The yolks should be dark yellow, with a greenish/gray tinge.

TASTING NOTES

Two things you can count on experiencing the moment the automatic doors slide open in any Taiwanese convenience store: a cheerful shout of *huanying* (welcome!) from behind the counter, and the distinctive soy sauce and black tea aroma of tea eggs wafting from the store's ready-to-eat section. The tea eggs will be in a crock pot (usually next to the steam tower containing warm buns, another Taiwanese convenience store staple) ready to be placed into waiting plastic bags with tongs, or slipped into a pocket on a chilly day. Already cracked during the cooking process, the shells should fall away easily. You'll make short work of the snack, eating the tan egg white and creamy yellow yolk in a few tasty bites.

● *by Joshua Samuel Brown*

YOU'LL NEED
500g (1lb) chicken heads
500g (1lb) chicken feet

For traditional style
1 tsp oil
1 cube chicken bouillon
spices of your choice
pinch of salt

For tasty style
6 tbs oil
2 medium onions, thickly
    sliced
2 green peppers, thickly
    sliced
4 medium tomatoes, thickly
    sliced
1 cube chicken bouillon
spices of your choice
pinch of salt

ORIGINS

During the apartheid years
in South Africa, farmers of
European origin favoured the
meatiest parts of the chicken.
The leftovers – like the heads
and the feet – were given to
workers, who adapted them
to their culinary needs, usually
for children. Although the key
ingredients are no longer free,
they are sold cheaply to locals.
That may of course change now
that Simba-brand potato
crisps come in walkie-talkie
chicken flavour too!

SERVES 6

SOUTH AFRICA

WALKIE-TALKIES

Walkie-talkies are gluten-full feet and protein-packed heads. Literally. Perhaps they're not the most appetising-looking stewed chicken parts, but in South African townships, walkie-talkies are low-priced, lip-smacking, pluck-giving delights.

METHOD

1 Wash the chicken heads and feet thoroughly. Place together in boiling water for about one minute to soften them.

2 Remove from the water (keep it boiling for traditional-style walkie-talkies) and then cut off the beaks, clean the feathers from the head and peel the tough outer layer of skin off the feet. If desired, pull out the toenails.

For traditional style

3 Place the cleaned heads and feet back in the boiling water. Add oil and a pinch of salt. Cook on medium heat for 10 minutes.

4 Add a cube of chicken bouillon and other spices to taste. Maintain medium heat for an additional 20 minutes (or 10 minutes for a less tender result). Drain and serve.

For tasty style

3 Heat 3 tbs oil in a frying pan over medium heat. Add the onions and a pinch of salt. Continually stir the onions, deglazing as necessary, until they are lightly browned.

4 Add another 3 tbs oil, the chicken heads and feet, green peppers, tomatoes, cube of chicken bouillon and any desired spices.

5 Cover and cook over a medium heat for 10 to 15 minutes, stirring from time to time. Remove and serve. Eat with cooked maize (South African 'pap').

TASTING NOTES

Township markets are always abustle, brimming with a wonder of sights, sounds and smells. Adding to the rumpus are walkie-talkies. Some are just boiled, with added salt and spices; others are stewed with onions, green peppers and tomatoes; lately, they are grilled too. Whatever the style, you stick the feet in your mouth toes first and then scrape the skin and meat off with your teeth. The rest can be chewed up for the bone marrow. It takes a bit of determined crunching, but not as much as required for the head, which gets eaten whole, except for the beak. ● *by Ethan Gelber*

ORIGINS

This method of coating chunks of mutton with a mixture of cumin, salt and chilli pepper before skewering and grilling them to perfection over a bed of coals reflects the tastes and traditions of central Asia, specifically the Uighur people of China's northwestern Xinjiang Province. Most purveyors of *yangrou chuan*, the variants of which are as countless as the country's billion-odd people, either hail from this region or are Hui (Chinese Muslims).

MAKES 12 SKEWERS

NORTHWESTERN CHINA, BEIJING & OTHER URBAN AREAS

YANGROU CHUAN

From the urban canyons of Beijing to the far-flung reaches of Kashgar, these grilled skewers of seasoned lamb unite migrant workers, party cadres and the nouveau riche alike.

YOU'LL NEED

12 skewers
500g (1lb) boneless leg of
  lamb
30ml (⅛ cup) vegetable oil
2 tbs ground cumin
2 tbs chilli pepper
salt and pepper, to taste

METHOD

1 If using bamboo skewers, soak them for an hour in water (to prevent them from burning) and prepare a charcoal grill or barbecue.

2 Cut the meat into small pieces about the size of a walnut.

3 Add about five to eight pieces of meat per skewer.

4 Put your oil on one plate, and mix the spices on a second.

5 Roll the skewers in oil first, then the spice mix.

6 Grill the skewers for about two to three minutes on each side. The meat should be cooked but not too dry.

TASTING NOTES

Imagine yourself on an evening stroll in urban China. Perhaps you're in one of Beijing's hutong neighbourhoods, or maybe on a side street off a busy avenue in Xi'an. The smell of smoky grilled meat and a trace of cumin wafts through the air. Approaching the grill (one small enough to be carried away should the police come calling), you see a fellow alternately fanning the coals and spinning skewers of meat, announcing in Mandarin: '*Yangrou chuan! Yi tiao yi kuai!*' ('Mutton kebabs! One yuan per stick!'). The presence of a small crowd buying up skewers as fast as the vendor can make them is a good sign. Order half a dozen – they're the perfect evening snack. ● *by Joshua Samuel Brown*

ORIGINS

Poland's communist era is, for the most part, hardly missed. However, one positive legacy that it did leave is *zapiekanka*. For one reason or another, this humble street food rose to prominence in the 1980s, when it became a popular snack as a delicious, inexpensive stomach-filler. No doubt it proved a handy energy booster for the strikers who finally brought down the communist regime at the end of the decade.

SERVES 1

POLAND

ZAPIEKANKA

When Poles need a quick snack, they head for the serving window of a *zapiekanka* stand. These long toasted rolls with succulent toppings are guaranteed to stave off hunger pangs.

YOU'LL NEED

200g (7oz) mushrooms
1 baguette
100g (¼lb) ham, thinly sliced
120g (4¼oz) edam (or any other hard cheese that melts easily)
ketchup
mayonnaise

METHOD

1 Cut the mushrooms into thin slices and then saute them over medium heat until cooked.

2 Cut the baguette lengthwise into two long pieces.

3 Layer the ham, cooked mushrooms and cheese on the flat surfaces of each piece.

4 Toast under a grill until the cheese has melted and the bread is crisp.

5 Smother with ketchup and mayonnaise, then serve.

TASTING NOTES

Decide first on the size of *zapiekanka* you want – some are up to 50cm (20in) long – then select the toppings. Although traditionally these were simple, the modern *zapiekanka* has lived up to its billing as the Polish pizza by taking on ever-more exotic elements. Once your order is served up, you'll experience the satisfying crunch of toasted bread, followed by the palate-pleasing combination of cheese, mushrooms, a tangy sauce and whatever other toppings you've chosen. Recently, *zapiekanka* outlets have faced competition from kebab shops, so it's become harder to find a dedicated *zapiekanka* creator. Ask a local for pointers and beware the microwave oven – unless you want a soggy, tasteless shadow of the real McCoyski. ● *by Tim Richards*

SWEET

In which we indulge in cinnamon sprinkles, honeyed berries, molten chocolate, gooey syrup, frozen custard and steaming, sweet spiced chai. Sweet-toothed readers beware: the world's most tempting treats await. →

ORIGINS

The health benefits of the açai berry were known to Amazon tribes for centuries. Other Brazilians began enjoying the fruit after doctors started to extol its virtues in the 1950s. By the 1970s, kiosks and juice bars in Rio were selling *açai na tigela* (açai in a bowl) made with frozen açai pulp: the time it took to transport açai from the Amazon to the coast meant the fruit would spoil if shipped fresh.

SERVES 1

COASTAL BRAZIL

AÇAI NA TIGELA

Based on the frozen pulp of the antioxidant-rich Amazonian superfood açai, this popular granola-and-syrup-topped kiosk treat is a delectable start to the day.

YOU'LL NEED

100g (¼lb) frozen açai pulp
1 banana
granola
generous squeeze of guarana syrup (or honey)
2 ice cubes

METHOD

1 Blend together half the banana, the frozen açai pulp, the guarana syrup and the ice cubes until fairly smooth. Avoid blending too long or the pulp will start to melt. Pour into a bowl.

2 Slice the remaining banana and add over the top of the fruit blend along with the granola and a further dollop of guarana syrup. Serve immediately.

TASTING NOTES

If you thought street food was unhealthy, greasy or the domain of labourers, think again. You could easily find yourself queuing for your *açai na tigela* alongside the bronzed Brazilian jet set. Reams have been written on the nutritional advantages of this little berry, but even if it were packed with more calories than a treble-cream doughnut, you'd still want to treat yourself to this. The berry's deep purple wells up in the bowl when blended and its dominant notes of blueberry and dark chocolate are the perfect complement to that creamy, crunchy combo of banana and granola. It's laced with caffeine-laden guarana syrup, meaning *açai na tigela* is a great way to get over the previous night's shenanigans. ● *by Luke Waterson*

Grant Hooker, who founded the BeaverTails company with his wife, Pam, says that his grandmother used to make a similar doughy treat –a yeasted, cracked-wheat pastry fried and topped with cinnamon and sugar – that Canadian and American farm families commonly prepared. The Hookers opened their first BeaverTails shop in Ottawa in 1980, and later trademarked the name.

MAKES 8

YOU'LL NEED
2 tsp dried yeast powder
¼ cup lukewarm water
1 tsp sugar
150g (5oz) plain (all-purpose) flour
150g (5oz) whole wheat flour
1 tsp salt
¼ cup warm milk
45g (1½ oz) butter, melted
1 egg
vegetable or canola oil, for deep-frying
cinnamon sugar, for serving

OTTAWA, ONTARIO, CANADA

BEAVERTAILS PASTRY

What's more Canadian than a beaver? A BeaverTail! Not the back end of the mammal, BeaverTails pastries are doughy snacks first fried up in Ontario and now found across Canada.

METHOD

1 Mix the yeast with the water and sugar in a small bowl and let stand for five minutes.

2 In a mixing bowl, sift both flours with the salt.

3 Make a well in the centre of the flour and add the yeast mixture, milk, butter and egg. Mix well.

4 Tip out the dough on to a floured surface and knead for about 10 minutes, until the dough becomes soft and elastic.

5 Set the dough aside in a lightly oiled bowl to rise until it is almost double in size.

6 'Knock back' the dough by punching the air out of it and kneading it a few times.

7 Divide and roll the dough into two balls, and continue until there are eight balls.

8 With a rolling pin, flatten each ball into an oblong, beaver-tail shape.

9 Heat the oil in a deep-fryer (or a saucepan filled with enough oil for deep-frying).

10 Fry the dough pieces, a few at a time, for a few minutes on each side, until golden.

11 Using a slotted spoon, take out the pastries, sprinkle with cinnamon sugar and serve immediately.

TIP *The original recipe is trademarked and remains a closely guarded secret, but this version comes pretty close to the real thing, especially when served straight from the fryer and doused with cinnamon sugar.*

TASTING NOTES

A cross between a doughnut and buttery cinnamon-sugar toast, BeaverTails mix savoury dough with sweet toppings. Many countries have similar snacks, but what distinguishes these is the wheaty pastry; it's more substantial than a fried bread made from white flour. And since they are always cooked to order, you can eat them while they're hot and slightly crisp. The best way to sample one is while ice skating along Ottawa's Rideau Canal, a waterway that freezes in winter to become the world's longest skating rink. The tasty snack not only fuels you up for skating or other outdoor activities during the freezing winters, it also warms up your hands as you balance the warm pastry on your napkin. ● *by Carolyn B. Heller*

ORIGINS

Bliny, being round, yellow and hot, emerged in ancient Slav pagan culture as a symbol of the sun's return after the ravages of winter. They then shifted their meaning after the emergence of the Orthodox Church to become a central presence in the celebration of Maslenitsa, Russian Holy Week. The fact that the modern blin remains similar to the pagan one is testament to its position in the Russian popular consciousness, not to mention its irresistible tastiness.

TASTING NOTES

At the height of the Russian winter, stepping into a warm bliny shop is like getting a big hug from an old friend. A queue of people stands in front of a counter of servers clutching frying pans, taking their time to choose their fillings. The bliny are then fried to order – when they finally arrive, that first bite of the hot, paper-thin pancake folded in a triangle, with the filling oozing out and demanding to be licked off sticky fingers, is the definition of comfort food. But more than that, it is the social aspects of the ritual that make it really stand out. Every walk of Russian life is here, popping in to tuck into a centuries-old snack. ● *by Matt Bolton*

MAKES 12-16 BLINY

RUSSIA

BLINY

A steaming-hot wafer-thin pancake, filled with anything from cherries and cream to salmon and caviar, the blin is a quick-fire way to the heart of Russia's street life.

YOU'LL NEED

heaping ¼ cup buckwheat flour
heaping ¼ cup plain (all-purpose) flour
⅓ tsp baking powder
¾ cup milk
⅓ tsp dried yeast powder
1 egg, separated
125g (4⅓oz) butter

METHOD

1 Sift together the buckwheat flour, plain flour and baking powder into a large bowl.

2 Mix the milk and yeast together, then beat in the egg yolk.

3 Add the liquid mixture to the flour and whisk into a smooth paste.

4 Whisk the egg white until it is in smooth peaks, then fold into the flour and yeast mixture.

5 Heat the butter in a frying pan, then add the batter a tablespoon at a time, until the pan is thinly covered. Fry until the surface begins to bubble, then flip and cook the other side.

6 Serve with a filling of your choice – try salmon and cream cheese or cherries and cream.

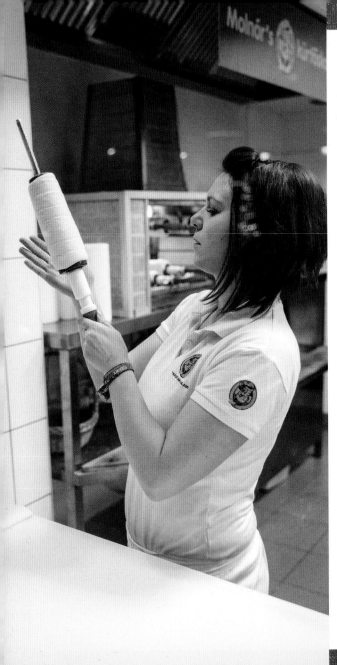

YOU'LL NEED

For the dough
1¾ cups plain (all-purpose)
  flour
2¼ tsp dried yeast powder
2 tbs sugar
⅛ tsp salt
3 tbs butter, melted
2 egg yolks (room
  temperature)
½ cup milk (room
  temperature)

For grilling
vegetable oil
butter, melted
sugar

For the topping
1 cup walnuts, ground
½ cup sugar
2 tsp cinnamon

ORIGINS

Traditionally made in the hills of
Transylvania, this treat spread
to market towns in the 19th
century, where peasants would
substitute pieces of dried corn
cob for wooden pins to wrap
the pastry. The name comes
from the cylindrical shape:
originally smoke from the wood
fires would escape through
the top, like a chimney. Today,
kürtöskalács are eaten at fairs
nationwide and are Hungary's
oldest and most beloved pastry.

HUNGARY

CHIMNEY CAKE

Chimney cake (*kürtöskalács*) is a cylindrical sugary roll of baked dough covered with walnuts, coconut and other toppings. It peels off in a spiral, making it fun to eat.

METHOD

1 Begin by preparing the dough. Mix the dry ingredients together in a large bowl.

2 Whisk the liquid ingredients together, and add them slowly to the dry ingredients. Stir the mixture until it forms a light dough.

3 Knead on a lightly floured surface for five to six minutes. Set aside and allow the dough to rise for 40 minutes.

4 Roll out the dough and slice it into a long ribbon.

5 Brush a wooden spit or rolling pin with the vegetable oil. Starting from one end, wrap the dough around the spit, making sure to tuck in the end so that the dough does not unwind.

The dough must be kept fairly thin (under 6cm or 2⅓in) as you stretch and wind it. Roll the wrapped spit on the counter in order to flatten it.

6 Brush the dough with the melted butter, then bake over an open flame for six minutes. Gradually sprinkle sugar on top until it changes to a darkish golden colour.

7 Mix the walnuts with the sugar and cinnamon. Paint another round of butter on to the dough, then roll the completed pastry in the walnut mixture.

8 Knock the mould on a table to release the cake, then stand upright to cool for several minutes. Serve warm.

TASTING NOTES

Eating the chimney cake is always a very social activity, and not just because it's regularly found at festival stalls. The cake's shape and consistency simply lends itself to sharing, making it easy for everyone in a group to reach their hand in and tear off a piece from a single roll – it's extremely popular with kids. Break off a piece of the chimney cake at one of the edges to watch it open and unravel like a spiral. The sugar has caramelised on the outside surface, beckoning your sweet tooth, while the soft underside might remind you of homemade sticky buns. It tastes akin to a cinnamon roll, but it's much more fun to eat.

● *by Roger Norum*

YOU'LL NEED

1 cup water
½ cup unsalted butter
1 cup plain flour
¼ tsp salt
3 eggs, lightly beaten
vegetable oil, for deep-frying
½ cup icing sugar, sifted
1 cup milk
200g (7oz) good quality
    dark chocolate, coarsely
    chopped

ORIGINS

The 'churro' sheep was a breed
known for the quality of its
wool. The Iberian shepherds
who looked after them were,
like most shepherds, only able
to carry the basics, which in
Spain was fried bread: simple
and easy to cook on the go.
Sugar was later sprinkled on
top of the dough and the shape
gradually evolved into its present
star-shaped form, meaning the
outside can crisp up while the
centre stays soft.

SPAIN

CHURROS

SERVES 8

What if you had a sugar-sprinkled, deep-fried pastry dipped into hot chocolate for breakfast every morning? Rolling out of bed sure would be a whole lot easier.

METHOD

1 Put the water and butter in a medium saucepan and bring to the boil, stirring until the butter melts.

2 While the liquid is still boiling, add the flour and salt and stir it swiftly with a wooden spoon until a dough forms. Continue to cook the dough for another minute then remove from the heat and transfer to an electric mixer bowl.

3 When the dough has cooled, add the lightly beaten eggs one at a time, making sure each one is fully incorporated before adding the next. Keep mixing until the dough appears smooth and not wet.

4 Spoon the dough into a piping bag fitted with a large (2.5cm or 1in), star-shaped nozzle.

5 In a deep saucepan, pour in vegetable oil to a depth of about 5cm (2in) and heat to 180°C (350°F). (If you don't have a thermometer, test the oil by dropping a small chunk of bread in. It should bubble to a golden brown in about 15 seconds.) Pipe lengths of dough (about 10cm or 4in is good) into the oil, cutting the dough off at the nozzle with a sharp knife.

6 Fry them until they're golden brown and crispy – they only take a minute or two – then remove with a slotted spoon and place on paper towel to drain. Dust with icing sugar.

7 To make the chocolate dipping sauce, simply combine the milk and chocolate in a saucepan over a medium heat and stir until the chocolate has melted and the sauce is smooth with a satin sheen.

TASTING NOTES

It's the sort of hangover that renders conversation impossible. Even thinking hurts. But then you catch the scent of sweet, frying dough. You stop, look around and spot the stall. A great vat is filled with boiling oil, and the fresh dough, pushed through a star-shaped nozzle, is plopped in. There is a delectable sizzle; no more than a minute passes before the crisp, piping-hot tubes are hauled out, drained and sprinkled with sugar. The first bite is red-hot but deeply addictive – a crunch then blissful softness. A few more and it's gone. The second churro disappears in record time. By the time the hot chocolate arrives, you're coming back to life, the grimace replaced by a sugared grin. ● *by Tom Parker Bowles*

1 cup milk

½ tsp vanilla extract

¾ cup plain (all-purpose) flour

⅛ tsp salt

2 tbs sugar

2 eggs

3 tbs unsalted butter, melted
  and cooled

melted butter for coating pan

ORIGINS

Crepes evolved from flatbreads
and get their name from the
Latin word for curled, *crispus*.
They originated in Brittany and
Normandy, where they were
prepared with the cheaper
local buckwheat flour. This
variety is now called a *galette*.
In sit-down creperies, *galettes*
are the savoury main course,
with crepes for dessert. Street
stands only use crepe batter,
regardless of the filling. On
Candlemas, it is considered
lucky to flip a crepe while
holding a coin in the left hand.

MAKES 8

FRANCE

CREPES

A venerable French icon, these paper-thin pancakes are sprinkled with sugar, stuffed with fruit or crammed with savoury fillings. On the street they're served folded to fit in your hand.

METHOD

1 In a small bowl, combine the milk and vanilla.

2 Sift the flour, salt and sugar together in a medium-sized bowl.

3 Make a well in the centre of the flour mixture. Add the eggs and one-third of the milk mixture to the well and whisk to gradually incorporate the dry ingredients.

4 Once smooth, whisk in the remaining milk and melted butter.

5 Leave the batter to rest at room temperature for 30 minutes. It should be as thick as heavy cream.

6 Heat a small flat-bottomed frying pan or crepe pan (first-timers should make sure to use a nonstick pan) over medium heat and brush it with a bit of melted butter, which should sizzle but not brown.

7 Pour a small amount of batter into the pan and tilt it to allow the batter to thinly cover the bottom.

8 When the bottom of the crepe is golden brown, flip it to cook the other side. Cook the remaining batter in the same way, re-buttering the pan only if the crepes begin to stick.

9 Sprinkle your crepes with icing (powdered) sugar, spread them with jam or stuff them with your favourite seasonal fruit.

TASTING NOTES

Waiting in line, you'll smell the carnival-sweet steam rising from the griddle as the crepe batter sizzles in melted butter. When you reach the window, you'll see the cook spread the batter with a few turns and a flick of the wrist, using a wooden spatula called a *rozell*. It's hard to resist biting into your crepe as soon as it's handed to you, folded in six. Nutella is a popular filling, but crepes go with just about anything, from lemon and sugar to ham and cheese; the textures are as variable as the garnish. Sweet crepes are a gooey, dessert-like treat. In savoury ones, the pancake layers create a mouth-watering contrast with the salty richness of the filling. ● *by Meredith Snyder*

ORIGINS

The origin of *daulat ki chaat* is lost in the mists of time, but it probably evolved as a way of using up a surplus of milk. Since it's a speciality closely associated with Old Delhi, where it's a popular street snack in winter, it's possible that the Mughal emperors were among the first to savour this ephemeral treat. Today, it's a touch of the divine, a contrast with the noisy bustle of the bazaars where it's usually found.

SERVES 8

DELHI, INDIA

DAULAT KI CHAAT

Comprised of milk, saffron and sugar and topped with
pistachios and sometimes silver leaf, this sweet, delightful
treat is as light as air and as heavenly as moonlight.

YOU'LL NEED

2¼ cups cream
8 cups milk
1 tsp cream of tartar
1 tsp rose water
1 cup caster sugar
25g (1oz) chopped pistachio
  nuts
saffron (optional)
varq (silver leaf) (optional)

METHOD

1 Blend the cream, milk and cream of tartar and then
refrigerate overnight.

2 The next day, add the rose water and 4 tsp of the caster
sugar to the mixture, then whisk well (by hand or with an
electric mixer).

3 Scoop the resulting foam in layers into serving bowls, adding
caster sugar between each layer. Beat the remaining milk to
continue creating foam, until all the milk is used up.

4 Chill, then serve with the pistachio pieces, saffron and *varq*
sprinkled on top.

TASTING NOTES

Daulat ki chaat is one of those dishes with a flavour and texture that are difficult to describe.
The first taste imparts a hint of butter, then the tongue detects the subtle flavour of saffron
followed by the pistachios, unrefined sugar and dried condensed milk sprinkled on top. The
initial impression soon fades to leave behind a hint of creamy sweetness, prompting you to
take another mouthful in order to recapture the heavenly sensation. Because *daulat ki chaat*
would collapse in high temperatures, it's only prepared in the cooler months. Its creators
also claim that the dish should stand overnight beneath the moonlight for best results, and
that the morning dew is essential for it to set correctly. ● *by Tim Richards*

YOU'LL NEED

310g (11oz) soybeans
water for soaking beans
8 cups water
1 tbs cornflour
1 tsp edible *terra alba* (ie
  food-grade gypsum or
  food-grade calcium sulfate,
  available from Chinese
  grocery stores)
280g (10oz) brown or white
  sugar
2 tbs ginger, finely sliced, or
  pandan leaves for flavouring
  (optional)
2 slices lemon or a dash of
  vinegar

ORIGINS

Tofu is believed to have originated sometime during the Han dynasty (206BC–AD220). As Buddhism spread across East Asia in later dynasties, tofu, a key staple for vegetarian monks and nuns, followed. It's incredible versatility (think pure white cubes swimming in a sea of explosively hot chillies or crispy deep-fried nuggets of joy) was surely no secret, and today *douhua*, just one of its many derivatives, can be found everywhere from China to Malaysia and the Philippines to Indonesia.

CHINA, SINGAPORE & TAIWAN

DOUHUA

Comprising soft tofu topped with sweet delights – ginger-spiked syrup, peanuts, sesame paste, coconut milk or red beans – *douhua* is a Chinese pudding found in various forms across Asia.

METHOD

1 Rinse the soybeans to clean them, then put them into a pot, adding enough water to cover the beans three times over. Soak the beans until they expand to roughly twice their original size (may take eight hours).

2 Drain the beans, then add six cups of fresh water. Process the soybean/water mixture thoroughly in a blender.

3 Use a cheesecloth to squeeze out the liquid (soy milk) into a pot. Discard the pulp left in the cloth.

4 Add ½ cup water to the soy milk in the pot and cook on low heat, stirring and scraping the bottom of the pot continuously, until it begins to boil and foam. Remove from the heat, then filter out the scum with a small sieve or cheesecloth.

5 Mix ½ cup water with the cornflour and *terra alba*.

6 Return the soy milk to the boil, then very quickly stir in the *terra alba* mixture.

7 Turn off the heat, being careful not to move the pot as this will disturb the setting. Cover and allow to sit for 30 minutes.

8 Meanwhile, make the syrup by boiling the sugar in a cup water (with the ginger or pandan leaves if desired) for 2–3 minutes. Add the lemon or vinegar and allow to cool.

9 Drain any scum off the set *douhua*. Add the syrup and serve.

TIP *You can spice things up with ground peanuts, sesame seeds, chocolate, or a smidgen of fresh ginger sprinkled on top.*

TASTING NOTES

This is all about the silken, almost liquid texture of the special super-soft tofu. It melts in the mouth a bit like panna cotta or a delicate egg-custard flan – you won't appreciate just how refreshing it tastes until you try it at the end of a long, hot summer day. *Douhua* used to be sold fresh from bikes, with wooden buckets attached to the back. This is less common today, but you'll still come across it everywhere in Asia, in stalls and restaurants alike, served with a range of optional sweet toppings so you can style it to suit your mood. ● *by Tom Parker Bowles*

YOU'LL NEED

⅔ cup sugar
2 large eggs
¼ cup evaporated milk
½ cup water
1 tsp vanilla extract
2 tbs melted butter
⅔ cup plain (all-purpose) flour
3½ tbs cornflour
1 tsp baking powder
2 tbs custard powder
cooking oil spray

ORIGINS

Gai daan tsai (little eggs) came into being in the middle of the 20th century after the People's Republic of China was established and the ensuing rush to the colony necessitated the creative use of limited culinary resources. One story goes that the batter was devised to make use of damaged eggs. Another has it that the egg-shaped waffle-maker compensated for a batter that itself lacked eggs. Even today, not all waffles include eggs – but the best do.

OLIVER LANTZENDÖRFER, SEET YING LAI PHOTOGRAPHY © GETTY IMAGES

HONG KONG, CHINA

EGG WAFFLE

These cakey puffs are distinguished in the world of waffles by their bite-size proportions: each circular waffle is made up of 30 egg-shaped puffs, held together by crispy batter.

METHOD

1 Cream the sugar and eggs in a large bowl.

2 Add the evaporated milk, water, vanilla extract and melted butter and mix together.

3 Sift the dry ingredients into the bowl, then stir in to form a smooth batter, free of lumps.

4 Cover and place in the fridge for 1–2 hours.

5 Heat a waffle iron until hot and spray it lightly with cooking oil.

6 Pour in the batter, filling the waffle iron to about three-quarters full.

7 Close the iron and swivel to coat both sides with batter.

8 Cook for two to three minutes on each side until the batter turns crispy and golden.

9 Place on a cooling rack for one minute, then eat while still hot.

TASTING NOTES

Amid the savoury dumpling and congee aromas wafting around Hong Kong, the whiff of a sweet egg waffle will hit you like a sepia-toned memory from grandma's kitchen. Then you'll see one. Waffle-sellers often have several skillets steaming away, ensuring that each customer receives the freshest waffle, rolled on a cooling tray and plonked in a paper bag. The perfect one is eaten hot: the outer 'egg shell' crispy and the yellow innards soft, chewy and barely there. It should be sweet, but not overly so, leaving a pleasant aftertaste. The size-to-heat maintenance ratio might make the rapid eating of 30 'eggs' slightly challenging, but the easy-to-tear-and-share proportions make it a snack that is best eaten among friends. ● *by Penny Watson*

ORIGINS

Some say Marco Polo rediscovered a predecessor to the iced dessert during his travels along the Silk Road and introduced it back to Italy upon his return. Others say Catherine de Medici took her knowledge of gelato to France, when she married Henri Duc d'Orléans. Oh, and Charles I was so obsessed with the stuff he had his own 'Royal Ice Cream Maker'. Wonderful stories all, but utterly without evidence to back them up.

ITALY

SERVES 12

GELATO

Essentially a frozen egg custard flavoured with myriad ingredients and served piled into a glass, cone or cup, proper gelato is simple, unadulterated bliss; love at first lick.

YOU'LL NEED

12 egg yolks, beaten
1½ cups sugar
6 cups milk
1 tbs grated orange or lemon peel

TIP *This is a basic custard-cream gelato recipe, from which you can create your own delicious flavours – think seasonal fruit, nuts, chocolate, coffee... You will get smoother results if you have an ice-cream maker, but making it by hand is just as good.*

METHOD

1 Place the egg yolks, sugar and three cups of milk in a large saucepan and whisk over a low heat, making sure not to cook the egg yolks and turn the whole lot into scrambled eggs. The mixture is ready when it sticks to the whisk.

2 Take it off the heat, whisk through the rest of the milk and the peel. Cover and chill overnight before transferring to your ice-cream maker to do the rest of the work. If you don't have an ice-cream maker, place a deep, durable baking dish in your freezer. When you've taken the mix off the heat and stirred through the remaining milk and peel, chill the mix over an ice bath before transferring to the chilled baking dish and into the freezer.

3 Check the mixture every 30 minutes – when it starts to freeze around the edges, stir the frozen parts into the rest. Continue this process over the next 2–3 hours. The key is to avoid icy crystals so whisking it at regular intervals will ensure you get a smooth, and not frosty, result.

TASTING NOTES

This is the taste of childhood that keeps on giving. But forget all those dreary modern imitators, largely 'air and fakery' in the words of Jane Grigson. For the true gelato experience, you want your custard fresh, flavoured with fruit purees made that morning. A proper gelateria delights the eyes as much as it does the taste buds. There's chocolate of the darkest hue, a bright green pistachio that dances across the tongue. You go for a scoop of delicate strawberry, and then another of almond and finally cassata Siciliana. The texture is delicate and beautifully balanced, the flavours exploding around the mouth like fireworks.

● *by Tom Parker Bowles*

2 tbs *gulaman* (grass jelly –
available from Asian markets)

2 tbs cooked tapioca pearls
in syrup

2 tbs cold custard

2 large glasses of ice cubes

2 tbs palm fruit in syrup
(available from Asian
supermarkets)

2 tbs *nata de coco* (immature
coconut flesh, available
from Asian markets)

2 tbs preserved jackfruit
(available canned from Asian
markets)

2 tbs sweetened red beans
(available canned from Asian
markets)

2 tbs canned chickpeas

⅔ cup evaporated milk

1 scoop of *ube* (purple yam)
ice cream (available from
Asian markets)

ORIGINS

The name means 'mixed
together' in Tagalog, and that's
just what this is – a mad mix of
every sweet ingredient the chef
could get his hands on. The
inspiration is widely accepted to
be Japanese *kakigori*, brought
to the islands by immigrant
farmers who pioneered modern
agriculture in the 1900s. This
may explain why the dish is
enjoyed so enthusias-tically
by Filipinos, whereas later
Japanese imports are tarnished
by association with WWII.

SERVES 1

THE PHILIPPINES

HALO HALO

The American sundae meets Asia's bounty in the Philippines' favourite dessert, a captivating combination of shaved ice and evaporated milk mixed with an edible rainbow of fruit, seeds and jellies.

METHOD

1 Ahead of time, prepare your grass jelly according to the packet instructions. Chop into small cubes.

2 Also prepare your tapioca pearls. Heat one cup of water to a boil and slowly add one tablespoon of dry tapioca pearls. Reduce the heat and stir gently until the pearls float to the surface. Simmer for 15 minutes on a medium heat then allow to stand for 15 minutes. Stir in a tablespoon of syrup and chill in the refrigerator.

3 You'll also need cold custard – follow your favourite recipe and chill in the refrigerator.

4 Next, make your shaved ice. Crush two large glasses of ice cubes in an electric blender – most modern blenders have a setting for crushing ice.

5 In a large sundae glass, pile in your grass jelly, tapioca, custard, palm fruit, nata de coco, jackfruit, red beans, and chickpeas.

6 Top up the glass with crushed ice and pour over the evaporated milk. Top with a scoop of purple yam ice cream (if you can't find it, normal ice cream is a perfectly acceptable substitute) and serve.

TASTING NOTES

There's something about halo halo that takes you back to being a kid at a birthday party. It's probably the rainbow colours and the infinite variety of embellishments and sprinkles. While the base of halo halo is straightforward – just shaved ice and evaporated milk – the accompanying ingredients are an intoxicating journey through tastes, scents and textures. What's that translucent lump? Could be jackfruit. Could be a palm seed. You'll only know by tasting. The black cubes? Probably seaweed jelly. Those white slivers? Maybe *nata de coco*. It's easy to spot the chickpeas and red beans, and the vivid purple scoop on the top is almost certainly *ube* (purple yam) ice cream, but you'll only find out for sure when you put the sweet sticky mixture in your mouth and embark on the journey. ● *by Joe Bindloss*

ORIGINS

Long-time vendors say *hotteok* was an instant hit with children when it first appeared in the 1960s. Sweet, warm and inexpensive, it was prized among kids accustomed to adversity as the country agonised through rapid industrialisation and autocratic governments. That duality of despair and delight, hunger and satisfaction etched into the national psyche and transformed a simple pancake into a cultural icon enjoyed by people of all ages.

YOU'LL NEED

For the dough

¼ cup warm water
1 tsp dried yeast powder
2 tbs brown sugar
1 cup whole wheat flour
¾ cup glutinous rice flour (sometimes called sweet rice flour)
½ tsp salt
½ cup milk (room temperature)
3 tbs vegetable oil

For the filling

¼ cup brown sugar
½ tsp cinnamon powder
2 tbs chopped peanuts, walnuts or almonds
1 tbs sesame seeds, lightly crushed
1 tbs sunflower seeds, lightly crushed

TASTING NOTES

There's a contagious excitement about *hotteok* that begins with the sticky, lingering aroma. Patrons jostle for position to admire the handiwork of the grandmothers who are churning out *hotteok* with factory-like precision. Once you've got one in your hand, the temptation to take a huge bite is almost overwhelming. Fight it – the molten sugar will burn your tongue. It's safer to start nibbling the top edge, which is where you'll find the sweet spot: the tender bread, caramelised sugar, and seeds and nuts combine to yield an earthy sweetness reminiscent of a crème brûlée. And as that sensation registers, you'll experience the moment of truth: *hotteok* isn't just a snack, it's 50 years of memories rolled into a pancake.

● *by Rob Whyte*

SOUTH KOREA

HOTTEOK

**Hotteok is a soft, chewy pancake with a nutty filling
that's packed with sugar, cinnamon and crunchy
goodness. Hot off the griddle, it's served in a paper cup.**

METHOD

1 Combine the water, yeast and 1 tbs sugar in a small bowl. Stir until dissolved. Set aside for 10 minutes.

2 Combine the wheat flour, rice flour, salt and 1 tbs sugar in a large bowl.

3 Add the yeast mixture to the dry ingredients. Gradually add the milk while mixing.

4 Use your hands to form a ball of dough.

5 Knead the dough for three minutes and then place it in a bowl and cover. Set aside in a warm spot and allow to rise for one to three hours or until the dough doubles in volume.

6 To make the filling, combine the sugar, cinnamon, nuts and seeds.

7 Punch down the dough and knead it again for one minute. Divide it into six equal pieces.

8 Use your hands to stretch out each piece of dough and make a flat circle about the size of a CD.

9 Make a small pocket in the centre and add 1 tbs of filling.

10 Fold the outside edges of the dough into the centre and form a ball.

11 Heat the oil in a frying pan over medium-high heat.

12 Put a dough ball into the hot pan and flatten it with a spatula or large wooden spoon.

13 Cook until golden brown, roughly two minutes on each side.

14 Once cooked, place the pancakes on paper towels to remove the excess grease. Serve hot.

YOU'LL NEED

1 cup dried *adzuki* beans (red beans)
½ cup granulated sugar
¼ tsp salt
2 cups ice per person
agar jelly, available from Asian supermarkets (or regular fruit jelly as a substitute)
attap chee (palm seeds) in syrup, available from Asian supermarkets
cendol (grass jelly), available from Asian supermarkets
canned creamed sweetcorn
sliced banana
rose syrup
evaporated or condensed milk
crushed peanuts

ORIGINS

Many nations claim to have invented shaved ice – Hawaiian snow cones, Sicilian granitas, Filipino halo halo, Japanese *kakigori* – but the Singapore/Malay version takes the concept to a whole new level. Possibly concocted in Singapore in the 1930s when ice machines first appeared, *ice kacang* translates to 'red bean ice'. Since then, the list of toppings has grown to include a dazzling array of ingredients that reflect the region's plantations: palm seeds, agar, peanuts and sweetcorn.

SINGAPORE & MALAYSIA

ICE KACANG

Singapore's best-loved pudding resembles an alien moonscape – rainbow colours, surreal shapes and other-worldly textures. Welcome to pimped-up shaved ice, Malay Straits style!

METHOD

1 Begin by preparing the beans. Soak one cup of *adzuki* beans overnight, then boil for 10 minutes.

2 Discard the first batch of liquid and add enough fresh water to cover the beans, along with the sugar and salt. Simmer until the beans are soft, then drain and chill. Alternatively, you can find sweetened red beans in cans in many Asian supermarkets.

3A To prepare the shaved ice, you can either go the easy route or the hard one. The easy way is to add the ice one cup at a time to a blender and blend at low speed until the crushed ice has an even texture. This creates a crunchier mix than classic *ice kacang*.

3B Alternatively, you can wash out an empty cardboard milk or juice carton, then fill it

with water and freeze. When the carton is frozen solid, peel off the cardboard, and shave the ice manually using a cheese grater that catches the shavings internally. Use a rapid back-and-forth motion and empty the ice shavings regularly into a pre-chilled bowl. Store in the freezer until the other ingredients are ready.

4 Prepare the agar jelly in advance and cut it into small cubes.

5 Place a handful of preserved palm seeds at the bottom of each bowl, then cover with layers of ice shavings, jelly, red beans, cendol, sweetcorn and banana.

6 Finish with a final flourish of ice shavings, then pour rose syrup and evaporated (or condensed) milk over the creation. Top with crushed peanuts and serve.

TASTING NOTES

Eating *ice kacang* is only part of the pleasure (it tastes like an explosion in a sweet shop); watching the blending of ingredients is half the fun. It's like a special-treat sundae of childhood, but in Malaysia and Singapore you can have it every day. When you finally sink your spoon into this fantasy creation, the first thing you notice is not the cold – well-prepared *ice kacang* should melt on the tongue like fresh snow – but rather the sweetness of the syrup, fruit and milk. Then the mining expedition begins. Textures and flavours pass like geological strata as you dig for the elusive treasure of the sweet, gelatinous palm seeds at the bottom of the bowl. *Sedap* (delicious)! ● *By Joe Bindloss*

ORIGINS

Jalebis probably originated in ancient Persia (where they were known as *zoolbia*), with the earliest literary record being 13th-century manuscripts. Documentation suggests the sweet first came to the Indian subcontinent at least 500 years ago with the Mughals. Local variations have made *jalebis* a standout among India's wildly colourful medley of *mithai* (sweets).

YOU'LL NEED

85g (3oz) plain (all-purpose) flour
1 tsp gram flour
½ tsp dried yeast powder
½ tsp sugar
½ tsp vegetable oil
100ml(3½fl oz) lukewarm water
vegetable or canola oil, for frying

For the sugar syrup

120g (4¼oz) sugar
½ cup water
pinch of cardamom powder
pinch of saffron
1 tsp lemon juice

TIP *A piping bag or a plastic bottle with a pointed nozzle is a neat and easy way of making the signature* jalebi *squiggle.*

TASTING NOTES

Biting into a squiggly *jalebi* can be described as nothing short of, well, orgasmic. The arousing interplay of textural experiences – from the crispy yet playfully chewy outer shell to the warm, sweet syrup that seeps out from within – is tempered with flirtatious hints of fragrant rosewater or *kewra* water (Pandanus syrup). After haggling in India's frenetic bazaars, nothing is quite as revivifying as the sugar hit of a *garam garam* (hot hot) *jalebi*. Half the fun is watching a street-side vendor swirl the batter and flip the frying sweets until both sides are honey brown. The *jalebis* are then plunged into a vessel of thick syrup before being popped on to a plate and handed to the hungry customer. ● *By Sarina Singh*

INDIA

JALEBIS

Visually and texturally tantalising, luscious *jalebis* – with their crunchy circular shells that ooze thick, gooey syrup – are the ultimate sugar fix and one of India's most-loved sweet treats.

METHOD

1 Put the plain and gram flours in a mixing bowl and add the yeast and sugar. Make a well in the centre.

2 Pour in the oil and water and mix until smooth. The texture should be slightly runny like pancake batter. Add more water if necessary. Pour the mixture into a plastic bottle or piping bag and set aside.

3 Put the syrup ingredients into a pot and bring to a rolling boil until the sugar melts and the mixture thickens slightly. Turn the heat to the lowest setting while frying the *jalebis*.

4 Heat 3.5cm (1½in) of oil in a frying pan. The oil is ready if a tiny amount of batter, dropped into the oil, sizzles and resurfaces without changing colour. If the batter colours straight away, the pan is too hot, so remove it from the heat for a few seconds.

5 Squeeze the *jalebi* batter into the oil in a pretzel shape about 5cm (2in) in diameter. Repeat two or three times, depending on the size of your frying pan, but do not crowd the pan.

6 Fry the *jalebis* until they are a golden honey colour on both sides.

7 Transfer the fried *jalebis* into the warm syrup and let soak for a few minutes.

8 Take out the *jalebis* and serve immediately.

ORIGINS

Supposedly, *martabaks* originated in India in the Middle Ages but spread to Saudi Arabia, Yemen, Malaysia, Thailand and Indonesia. *Muttabaq* is Arabic for 'folded', however, so many believe the *martabak* spread eastwards from the Middle East. It was possibly Indonesia's role as a heavyweight cocoa producer that led to the chocolate version becoming indispensable here.

YOU'LL NEED

For the dough

1½ cups coconut milk
1 tsp dried yeast powder
¾ cup sugar
2 cups plain (all-purpose) flour
2 eggs, beaten
150g (5oz) granulated sugar
¼ tsp bicarb soda (baking soda)
vanilla extract
butter
olive oil

For the filling

salted butter at room temperature (must be soft and spread easily)
condensed milk
dark chocolate sprinkles
granulated sugar
peanuts, finely chopped
sesame seeds

mild cheese, grated

TASTING NOTES

Martabak manis are usually made before your eyes. First, out comes the pancake: its own preparation requiring an art to keep the edges brown but not burnt, the centre of the batter cooked, still fluffy and none too heavy, and the whole thing easily taken from the pan. For the most fulfilling experience, order the special chocolate-and-cheese flavour. Slatherings of butter and condensed milk get dark chocolate sprinkles, chopped peanuts and seeds added on one half and cheese on the other. Because the pancake this happens on is still hot, fillings have time to gel in a gluttonous goo before the *martabak manis* are folded and devoured.

● *by Luke Waterson*

MAKES 5
PANCAKES

INDONESIA

MARTABAK MANIS

Although this folded coconut-and-yeast pancake is celebrated across the Middle East and Southeast Asia, it's Indonesia where butter-enrobed *martabaks* have reached their most chocolatey, cheesy pinnacle.

METHOD

1 Warm up the coconut milk over low-medium heat until bubbling.

2 Let it cool, then mix in the yeast. Stir well until the mixture has a frothy appearance. Set aside for five to ten minutes.

3 Mix the sugar and flour in a separate bowl. Create a well in the centre and pour in the beaten eggs.

4 Mix until smooth, then add the frothy coconut milk and mix again. Add the granulated sugar, bicarb soda and a few drops of vanilla extract and set aside for 15 minutes.

5 Meanwhile, prepare the filling ingredients so that they are easily accessible.

6 Heat a wide cast-iron pan with butter and a little olive oil to make the grease go further.

7 When the oil is hot, turn down the heat and add one-fifth of the mixture. Ideally, you should have a pancake that is 2cm to 3cm (¾in to 1¼in) thick.

8 Wait for the surface to dry and the outer edge to brown, then remove from the heat and place on a board (don't flip the pancake).

9 Repeat with the remaining batter to make five pancakes.

10 Cut the pancakes in half. Spread butter on both sides, then add the condensed milk.

11 To make a chocolate *martabak*, add the chocolate sprinkles, a dash of granulated sugar, the chopped peanuts and sesame seeds to one half.

12 For a cheese *martabak*, add the grated cheese to the other half.

13 Fold each half over and smear the outside with a glaze of butter and condensed milk to finish.

ORIGINS

For thousands of years, milk (often buffalo's) was heated with various spices and jaggery in traditional ayurvedic healing formulas. At the same time, tea, also considered a herbal remedy, was being drunk in pockets of what is now India. But it wasn't until the British East India Tea Company created vast tea plantations in the 19th century and marketed the product domestically that what we now know as masala chai was born. And what a treat it is too.

MAKES 1 CUP

INDIA

MASALA CHAI

Warm, spiced milky tea is the perfect 5pm boost. The locally grown tea and spices are boiled to strong, sweet perfection at the fairy-light-bedecked chai-*wallah* stall.

YOU'LL NEED

½ cup water
2.5cm (1in) piece of ginger, crushed or chopped
3–4 cardamom pods, ground
2.5cm (1in) stick dalchini, crushed
2 leaves lemongrass, chopped (optional)
dash of black pepper (optional)
1 whole clove (optional)
1 heaping tsp Assam (CTC) tea
½ cup milk

METHOD

1 Put the water, spices and tea in a pot and bring to a boil. The milk must not be added at this point: the ginger will cause it to curdle.

2 Once boiling, add the milk and allow it to heat or boil, then turn off the heat immediately. Let it sit for a minute or two before straining it into cups if you like a stronger brew.

3 Some families only add the tea after turning off the heat; they then allow it to steep for a few minutes. Boiling the tea makes the taste stronger but supposedly increases the caffeine content while diminishing its beneficial antioxidant properties. How you do it is up to you.

TASTING NOTES

Rush hour for chai-*wallahs* (chai vendors) is twilight, as people pause on their way home from work or the market. The elaborate counter has multiple gas stoves, lots of ancient-looking brass and stainless-steel vessels and is watched over by an image of the goddess Laxmi, a smudge of sandalwood on her forehead. The tea is steeped with sugar, spices and milk in a large pot, then poured through a cotton strainer into surprisingly dainty glasses. The *dalchini* (cassia, or Indian cinnamon) gives the strong tea body, the cardamom provides the perfume and the *adrak* (ginger) gives it bite – which the milk and sugar soften. The evening seems to soften, too, and one more cup puts the day to rest. ● *by Amy Karafin*

ORIGINS

Paan goes back 5000 years, when kings and queens had special paan attendants. The combination of *supari* (areca or betel nut) and betel leaf was thought to have healing, digestive and relaxant properties. Over time it absorbed more ingredients – from spices to sweets to silver leaf. Plain paan picked up chewing tobacco, now the most popular form, as the red spit stains covering India's streets demonstrate.

YOU'LL NEED

slaked-lime paste
kattha paste
1 betel leaf (kept moist)
preserved dates
sugar-coated fennel seeds (or
    normal fennel seeds if not
    available)
toasted coconut flakes
cardamom powder or
    cardamom pod
'Star'-brand powder, if
    available (a special blend of
    sweet, aromatic flavours)
gulkand
1 maraschino cherry
1 whole clove (optional)

INDIA

MITHAA PAAN

Everyone looks bewildered when they first taste
mithaa paan (sweet paan), a betel leaf filled with powders,
pastes, seeds, fruit and mystery that is eaten after meals.

METHOD

1 Place a dribble of the slaked-lime and kattha pastes on the betel leaf; spread around the leaf and blend. (In a pinch, substitute with honey.)

2 Add the preserved dates and sprinkle with sugar-coated fennel seeds, toasted coconut, cardamom powder or pod, and Star powder.

3 Spoon on a smidge of gulkand, and top with a maraschino cherry.

4 Fold the betel leaf into a triangle, covering the mixture with three flaps of leaf. Bind together with the clove or a toothpick. *Mithaa paan* can be refrigerated for a few hours if necessary but tastes best fresh.

TASTING NOTES

You'll see them all over India by the roadside, near restaurants and lunch spots: *paan-wallahs*, sitting cross-legged amid stacks of shiny betel leaves and a hundred stainless-steel containers, jars, tins and boxes. They work like scientists, taking a scoop, a sprinkle or a pinch of each ingredient, working deftly and in order, stopping only to ask for your preferences. The finished product is a giant wad that fills the mouth and quickly begins its symphony of textures and exotic flavours – the smooth leaf, the spicy clove and fennel, the gooey dates and *gulkand*, the sweet coconut, the crunchy sugar-coated seeds and (if you choose) the hard *supari*. Eating it is the perfect ending to a meal. ● *by Amy Karafin*

Believed to have been imported by Arabs in the 18th century, Moroccan *sfenj* were originally available from stands alongside those where roasted lamb's head (a breakfast complement) was prepared in the weekly souks of major population centres. Today, as one of Morocco's street-food staples, *sfenj* are found at most hours of the day throughout the country, although they are customarily noshed first as a morning treat and then again in the late afternoon.

TASTING NOTES

Morocco's labyrinthine medinas see brisk business, the constricted byways a haphazard jumble atumble with goods and food. Amid the eye-popping and energy-sapping commotion, *sfenj* are a perfect quick boost. They should always be ordered fresh, both because they're best that way and because you'll be able to witness their preparation. While not difficult to cook, *sfenj* can be very hard to get right. There's much to be learned from deft handlers – always men – including shaping the wet dough, getting it into the oil intact and fishing the fried results out with long skewers. The eating, though, is gratifyingly easy: when sweetly garnished, *sfenj* are light confections of which just one is rarely enough. ● *by Ethan Gelber*

MOROCCO

SFENJ

As croissants are to the French, so are *sfenj* to Moroccans. Eaten hot and sometimes sprinkled with sugar, these uniquely spongy, deep-fried pastry rings are essentially doughnuts gone pro.

YOU'LL NEED

1½ tsp dried yeast powder
½ cup lukewarm water
2½ cups plain (all-purpose) flour, sifted
1 tsp salt
vegetable oil
toppings of your choice
  – sugar and honey, for example

METHOD

1 Add the yeast to ¼ cup of lukewarm water. Set aside for a few minutes.

2 In a large mixing bowl, combine the sifted flour, salt and yeast water and then stir in another ¼ cup water.

3 Knead the mix (being careful not to add too much more flour) until the dough is sticky and stretchy. Place in a cloth-covered bowl and set aside in a warm spot for 2–4 hours.

4 When the dough is light, bubbly and has doubled in size, heat the vegetable oil in a frying pan.

5 Keeping your hands wet, lightly knead the sticky dough (keeping as many of the air pockets as possible) and divide into 12 pieces.

6 Using your palms, roll each piece into a ball and then, with your thumb, make a hole in the middle. Stretch the dough a bit to make a ring.

7 When the oil is hot, slip the rings into it, but don't overcrowd the pan. Fry each ring for two to four minutes per side or until golden brown.

8 Remove from the oil and drain on a paper towel. Serve hot.

GLOSSARY

açai Açai is the grape-like fruit from a palm native to Central and South America. The pulp is made by removing the flesh from the seed, freezing then mashing it.

adobo seasoning Adobo seasoning is a mix of spices and herbs used for marinating meat. The mix varies considerably from region to region throughout the Americas.

adzuki bean This is a legume common in east Asia and India (where it's known as *chori*). It's usually eaten in sweet dishes.

agar jelly Agar jelly is made from agar, an algae or seaweed extract – it's basically a vegetarian equivalent to gelatin.

aji limo This is a medium-hot Peruvian chilli.

ajvar *Ajvar* is a Croatian/Serbian red capsicum (pepper) relish.

amba Iraqi-style mango chutney.

amchur *Amchur* is a powder used as a souring agent in Indian cooking. It's made from dried, ground green mangoes. You can replace it with lemon/lime juice or tamarind water if you need to.

aonori An edible seaweed, often used as a seasoning.

arborio rice Arborio is a short-grain rice with a high starch content, often used in risottos.

Similar types of rice include Carnaroli and Vialone Nano.

Assam (CTC) tea A machine-processed Assam tea, usually best consumed with milk and other flavourings and sweeteners.

atta Atta flour is a hard-wheat flour. Doughs made with this flour can be rolled thin yet retain their integrity. Substitute with plain (all-purpose) flour if need be.

attap chee Immature fruit of the attap palm. Lychee could replace it.

baladi An heirloom eggplant, but can also refer to a dish prepared with them.

banana leaves The leaves of the banana tree, often used to wrap food while cooking. Available frozen if not fresh in Asian and Hispanic grocery stores. Use aluminium foil for wrapping the food otherwise.

bee hoon noodles Rice vermicelli noodles.

belacan Shrimp paste – pungent and salty. Use anchovies mashed with a little water as a replacement.

betel leaf A vine leaf, common to much of Asia.

bijao leaf A leaf used for wrapping foods while cooking. Use banana leaves or aluminium foil in its place.

bird's eye chilli A small chilli, technically medium in heat, but more than hot enough for most people.

buckwheat flour As the name suggests, flour made from buckwheat (which isn't wheat at all). It's a distinctly grey flour but, colour aside, can be replaced by plain (all-purpose) flour.

caciocavallo A cheese made in the fashion of mozzarella, but aged into a hard cheese. Substitute with provolone.

candlenuts A nut used to thicken Asian soups and curries. Try almonds, cashews or macadamias as replacements. If you find candlenuts (Asian grocery stores stock them), they must be cooked before eating them.

cendol An Asian sweet drink/desert, usually made with coconut cream, shaved ice and green, gelatinous threads made from rice flour.

cha lua A pressed meat, made from finely ground pork, not unlike baloney or devon in appearance. Commonly available in Vietnamese grocery stores.

chana dhal Split, dried chickpeas (garbanzo beans).

Chinese chives Also known as garlic chives. Use chives as a mild substitute.

Chinese sausage A sweet, dried pork sausage. Not easily replaced, but a very mild, aged salami could offer a similar consistency if not the taste.

chorizo A Portuguese or Spanish pork sausage, varieties ranging from mild to spicy. It is dry-cured, like a salami, and can be eaten uncooked. Substitute with pepperoni.

clam juice The stock produced from cooking clams. Available tinned. Substitute with fish stock.

cremini mushrooms Similar to a Swiss brown or portobello, both of which could be used as a substitute.

daikon A large, tubular, white radish, mild in flavour. Substitute with jicama or red radish (which is more pungent).

dalchini Cassia bark – a cinnamon-like spice. Use cinnamon in its place.

dendê oil Palm oil, though distinct from most cooking oils in its deep red colour. Use peanut oil in place of it (but you'll lose the red hue the oil imparts).

dried corn husks Used for wrapping foods, especially tamales. Substitute with banana leaves or aluminium foil.

dried flat rice noodles Also known as flat rice stick noodles. Easy to find in an Asian grocery store. Other rice noodles could be used as a substitute.

galangal A rhizome, similar in appearance to ginger, though darker. Ginger can be used in its place, but it is much milder than galangal.

garam masala A sweet blend of spices – cardamom, cloves, cumin, pepper, among others.

gari A mildly sour-tasting flour made from fermented, roasted cassava. Difficult to substitute for taste, but plain cassava flour is an option.

ghee Clarified butter.

glutinous rice flour Ground glutinous rice used in Asian deserts and as a thickener. Tapioca flour can be used as a substitute.

gram flour Ground chickpeas (garbanzo beans), also known as besan flour.

green mango Unripened mango.

green papaya Unripened papaya.

guarana syrup An extract of guarana mixed with sugar syrup.

guizador Peruvia in term for stewed turmeric. See turmeric.

gulkand Rose-petal jam from northern India and Pakistan.

habañero chilli A hot chilli, in the range of bird's eye chillies though somewhat hotter.

hoisin sauce A sweet, thick, dark sauce predominantly used in savoury cooking.

holy basil A pungent Asian herb with notes of anise, pepper and mint. Substitute with Thai basil or sweet basil along with some mint.

jaggery A caked sugar made from dehydrated sugar cane juice. Palm sugar is darker but can be used as a substitute. Dark brown sugar is a further alternative.

jicama A vaguely potato-looking tuber, especially when peeled. Eaten raw, it's crunchy and strangely juicy.

katsuobushi Dried, fermented and smoked tuna, often in flakes. Also known as bonito flakes, it's used as a condiment.

kattha An astringent paste extracted from an acacia tree. A common ingredient in paan.

kimchi Pickled, fermented cabbage – a Korean staple.

laksa leaves A weirdly metallic tasting mint, with strong pepper notes. Use mint and coriander as a substitute. Also known as Vietnamese mint.

Maldive fish flakes Dried and smoked bonito tuna, more splinters than flakes. Substitute with Japanese bonito flakes (*katsuobushi*).

masa harina A flour made from hominy (hulled corn kernels).

Mexican-style vinegar-based hot sauce Many brands (eg Valentina, El Yucateco), but Tabasco is perhaps the most widely known.

New Mexico green chillies Mild green chillies.

palm sugar Sugar made from the sap of the palm tree. Use dark brown sugar in its place.

pandan leaves Long leaves from the pandan plant, used as a colouring and flavouring in Southeast Asian cuisine.

plantains Related and similar in appearance to the banana, but needs to be cooked – often used in savoury dishes.

poblano chillies A ubiquitous Mexican chilli, it's mild (usually) and used in a variety of ways. Also known as ancho chilli in its dried form.

pomegranate molasses A thick,

dark, tart sauce made from reduced pomegranate juice. Use pomegranate or cranberry juice as a substitute.

provola A small-sized variant of provolone cheese, which is a semi-hard, cow's milk cheese. You can use fontina or asiago in place of it.

puffed rice Rice grains that have been heated under pressure. Kind of like Rice Bubbles/Krispies, but unsweetened.

queso anejo An aged goat or cow's milk cheese. Use romano or perhaps a mild goat's milk cheese in its place.

red Asian shallots A small red/pink onion, mild and somewhat sweet. Shallots are a fine substitute.

red curry paste A blend of dried red chillies, galangal, lemongrass, coriander root, garlic, shrimp paste, among other spices. A Thai staple. Available pre-made in Asian grocery stores.

rose syrup Rose syrup is a sweetened rose water, which itself is by-produced during the extraction of rose oil from rose petals. Use rose essence or rose water in its place.

salted radish Salted and preserved daikon radish. Available in Asian grocery stores.

sambal belacan A chilli paste made by blending together chillies, shrimp paste, lime and

sugar. It's pungent and spicy. If you don't have shrimp paste, you could use anchovies to make it yourself. Or buy it ready-made from an Asian grocery store.

Sarawak laksa paste Quite different to the more common laksa pastes, this paste features sambal belacan, tamarind, garlic, galangal and lemongrass. Asam (aka Penang) laksa paste could be used in its place.

sawtooth coriander leaves A long leafed herb, serrated as the name suggests. It can be replaced with coriander.

scotch bonnet chillies A hot chilli common in the Carribbean. It can be replaced with habanero.

semolina flour A hard wheat flour made from durum wheat. It is higher in gluten than plain (all-purpose) flour, but you could use thise in its place (the result will be different though).

sev A crispy, noodle-like, Indian snack.

shiitake mushrooms Also known as Chinese mushrooms, these are commonly available dried in Asian grocery stores – soak them in hot water for half an hour before using them.

shiso leaves A mint-family herb used throughout Asia. Mint can be used as a substitute.

shito A Ghanian sauce made from dried fish, oil, chilli, garlic, tomato and a variety of spices.

shrimp paste Also known as belacan, this is a pungent and salty paste used as a base for curries and other sauces. Use anchovies mashed with a little water as a replacement.

slaked-lime paste Calcium oxide mixed with water. You must use food-grade calcium oxide (also known as lime – like what you find in whitewash).

snake beans The pod of a climbing vine, the snake bean is unrelated to the common bean, but green beans can replace them. You'll need about four green/string beans for every snake bean.

star anise A star-shaped spice readily available in Asian grocery stores. Anise seed can be used as a substitute.

'Star'-brand powder 'Star'-brand powder is a feature of the spice collection of almost every paan-wallah. Difficult to replace, but if you find it, your *mithaa paan* will take you to the streets of Mumbai in a flash!

sticky rice Also known as glutinous rice. It's a short-grained Asian rice that becomes quite sticky when cooked. Try arborio rice or some other risotto rice as a replacement.

strong white flour Also known as bread-making flour, it has a higher gluten content than plain (all-purpose) flour.

sumac A generally ground spice made from the dried fruit of the sumac shrub.

supari Areca nut, chewed with betel for its stimulant effects. It can have a variety of negative physiological and neurological effects.

tahini paste Sesame seed paste.

tamarind concentrate Also known as tamarind paste, this is the pulp of the tamarind pod deseeded and ready to use. It's sour and only slightly sweet. Use lemon juice for a souring effect in its place.

tamarind paste see *tamarind concentrate*

tamarind pulp The pulp of the tamarind pod, usually available in blocks from Asian grocery stores. It will have the stony black seeds as well, which would need to be removed (usually after soaking the pulp in hot water for a while).

tamarind water The watered-down, deseeded pulp from the tamarind pod.

tapioca starch Tapioca flour, a common thickening agent. Use glutinous rice flour in its place.

terra alba Food-grade gypsum for setting soy-milk into tofu.

Thai basil Milder than holy basil, more pungent than basil – but basil can be used as a substitute.

turmeric A rhizome like ginger, usually smaller, and beneath the dull orange peel, you'll find brilliant gold. Available fresh in Asian grocery stores, and as a ground spice almost everywhere.

twarog cheese Also known as quark, this is a soft, unaged cheese. It's generally a cooking cheese. If you can't find it, try cottage cheese in a pinch.

Vegemite A spread made from yeast extract. It's sharp and pungent, deep black and smooth. It's an Australian staple. Irreplaceable (but use Marmite if you must).

Vietnamese mint A weirdly metallic tasting mint, with strong pepper notes. Use mint and coriander as a substitute. Also known as laksa leaf.

zapallo squash An enormous type of pumpkin/squash. Replace with any available pumpkin/squash.

zomi Ghanian word for palm oil.

AUTHORS

TOM PARKER BOWLES is a food writer with an ever-expanding gut. He has a weekly column in *The Mail on Sunday*, as well as being Food Editor of *Esquire*. He is also a Contributing Editor to *Departures* magazine. His first book, *E is for Eating: An Alphabet of Greed* (2004) was an opinionated romp through the world of food. His next, *The Year of Eating Dangerously* (2006) explored the more weird and exotic delicacies of the world. And his third, *Full English: A Journey Through the British and Their Food* was published in 2009 and won the Guild of Food Writers 2010 award for best work on British food. *Let's Eat* (2012) is a collection of his favourite recipes, gathered from around the world and recreated in his own kitchen. *Let's Eat Meat* (2014) is filled with recipes for meat… although it's all about eating less meat, but better quality.

Tom is also known for co-presenting *Market Kitchen* on Good Food Channel from 2007 to 2010, and is a judge of *The Hotplate* on Australia's Channel 9. To counteract all that eating, he once joined a gym, but sadly, it disagreed with his delicate constitution.

Abigail Hole Writer on four editions of Lonely Planet *India*, and enthusiastic researcher of the sumptuous, tangled flavours of *Dilli ki chaat* (Delhi street food).

Amy Karafin Lonely Planet *India* co-author, former resident of Dakar, Accra and Bombay, and master scout of dirt-cheap, vegetarian food the world over.

Austin Bush Writer of Thai food blog www.austinbushphotography.com, food writer for guidebooks and magazines including *Saveur*, *Travel + Leisure Southeast Asia*, *Chile Pepper*, and *DestinAsian*.

Brett Atkinson Habitual street food explorer, craft beer hunter, and cookery-class participant from Myanmar and Malaysia to Hanoi and Istanbul.

Bridget Gleeson writes for Lonely Planet's South America guides. She has a weakness for Argentinian *choripán*, preferably piled high with chimichurri.

Carolyn B. Heller A Vancouver-based travel and food writer who has eaten her way across five continents.

Celeste Brash Contributor to *The World as a Kitchen*, writer of food sections for Lonely Planet guidebooks and lonelyplanet.com and erstwhile professional cook.

Daniel Savery Raz Tel Aviv-based author who devoured Europe for *A Place in the Sun* magazine and often hunts for hummus. See www.danscribe.com.

Daniel Robinson Author of food reviews – and Lonely Planet guides – to culinary hot-spots such as France, Malaysia, Tunisia, Cambodia and Israel.

Duncan Garwood A dedicated fan of southern Italian food who has written for *Olive* magazine and co-authored Lonely Planet's *Sicily* guide.

Emily Matchar Culture and food writer for magazines and newspapers, and co-author of more than a dozen Lonely Planet guides.

Ethan Gelber Contributor to various Lonely Planet publications, editor-in-chief of www.thetravelword.com and passionate food lover.

Gregor Clark Co-author of Lonely Planet guides including *Brazil*, *South America on a Shoestring* (Uruguay) and *Italy*.

Jessica Lee Guidebook author and tour leader in the Middle East and North Africa, and avid Levantine cuisine foodie, still searching for the perfect hummus.

Joe Bindloss Former food critic for *Time Out*'s restaurant guides, specialising in food from Southeast Asia, China, Korea and the Indian subcontinent, and current Lonely Planet Destination Editor.

Johanna Uy Food writer and blogger at www.thehappydiner. wordpress.com.

Joshua Samuel Brown writes about travel and food for Lonely Planet. When not on the road in Taiwan, Singapore or Belize, he's eating food from trucks in Portland, Oregon. Follow him @josambro.

Luke Waterson Long-time Latin American traveller and ceviche sampler, Andes obsessive, author for Lonely Planet's *Peru*, *Ecuador*, *Mexico* and *Cuba*, culinary travel writer for the *Independent*, and for Lonely Planet's food titles.

Matt Bolton One-time senior staff writer at *Lonely Planet Magazine* UK, and a sucker for anything hot, flat and fried.

Matt Phillips loves food and has walked many a street to find it, indulging in everything from deep fried tarantulas to springbok biltong and bunny chow.

Megan Eaves is a New Mexican travel writer living in London; currently a Destination Editor for Lonely Planet. Will eat anything, but takes a special shine to food in dumpling form and knock-your-head-off spice.

Meredith Snyder Spent her childhood helping out in the kitchen and sampling street food in Paris; her travel writing has appeared on the web at BBC Travel and Vagabondish.com.

Michael Kohn Author or co-author on more than 15 Lonely Planet titles, freelance correspondent for BBC, and fan of spicy snacks from Central Asian bazaars.

Paul Clammer Regular visitor to Morocco since 1994 – first as traveller, then as tour guide and currently as guidebook author.

Penny Watson Contributor to *The Age Cheap Eats* guide, Sydney Morning Herald Good Food, South China Morning Post Food & Wine, and full-time glutton.

Rob Whyte Co-author of Lonely Planet's Korea, South Korea resident and *hotteok* enthusiast.

Roger Norum and Strouchan Martins Food and travel writers for various magazines including *Olive*.

Sarah Baxter Associate editor of *Wanderlust* travel magazine, contributor to Lonely Planet books and national newspapers, and Cornish pasty lover.

Sarah Reid is a travel journalist, Lonely Planet editor and eternal globetrotter. She has sampled the classic foodie delights of more than 70 countries.

Sarina Singh Contributor to Lonely Planet's *Out to Eat* series and co-author of dozens of other LP books.

Tim Richards Travel writer who has written about foreign food delights for many publications (see iwriter.com.au); and amateur dukkah connoisseur.

Trent Holden covers mainly African and Asian destinations for Lonely Planet. Currently based in London, in between travels he also freelances as a food and live-music reviewer. Follow his travels @hombreholden.

Will Gourlay Writer, researcher and inveterate traveller to Turkey, the Balkans and the Middle East, often found loitering at streetside charcoal grills.

Zora O'Neill Co-author of *Forking Fantastic! Put the Party back in Dinner Party* and blogging at Roving Gastronome (rovinggastronome.com).

INDEX

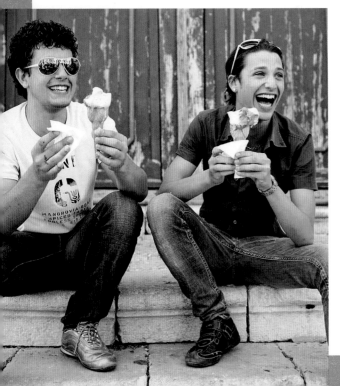

© TIM E WHITE

The World's Best Street Food

March 2016
Published by Lonely Planet Publications Pty Ltd
ABN 36 005 607 983
90 Maribyrnong St, Footscray,
Victoria, 3011, Australia
www.lonelyplanet.com
10 9 8 7 6 5 4 3 2 1

Printed in China
ISBN 978 1 76034 065 0
© Lonely Planet 2016
© Photographers as indicated 2016

Managing Director Piers Pickard
Associate Publisher Robin Barton
Commissioning Editor Jessica Cole
Art Director Daniel Di Paolo
Layout Designer Hayley Warnham
Cover Illustrator Muti – Folio Art
Editors Lucy Doncaster, Christina Webb
Pre-Press Production Nigel Longuet
Print Production Larissa Frost
Thanks to Lester Kaganzi
Written by Abigail Hole, Amy Karafin, Brett
Atkinson, Bridget Gleeson, Celeste Brash, Daniel
Savery Raz, Daniel Robinson, Duncan Garwood,
Emily Matchar, Ethan Gelber, Jane Ormond,
Jessica Lee, Joe Bindloss, Johanna Uy, Joshua
Samuel Brown, Luke Waterson, Matt Bolton, Matt
Phillips, Megan Eaves, Meredith Snyder, Michael
Kohn, Paul Clammer, Penny Watson, Rob Whyte,
Roger Norum, Sarah Baxter, Sarah Reid, Tim
Richards, Trent Holden, Will Gourlay, Zora O'Neill

Lonely Planet Offices

Australia
Level 2 & 3, 551 Swanston Street,
Carlton 3053, Victoria
Phone 03 8379 8000 Fax 03 8379 8111
Email talk2us@lonelyplanet.com.au

USA
150 Linden St, Oakland, CA 94607
Phone 510 250 6400 Toll free 800 275 8555
Fax 510 893 8572
Email info@lonelyplanet.com

Europe
240 Blackfriars Road, London, SE1 8NW
Phone 020 3771 5100 Fax 020 3771 5101
Email go@lonelyplanet.co.uk

Although the authors and Lonely Planet have taken
all reasonable care in preparing this book, we make
no warranty about the accuracy or completeness of
its content and, to the maximum extent permitted,
disclaim all liability from its use.

Paper in this book is certified against the Forest Stewardship
Council™ standards. FSC™ promotes environmentally
responsible, socially beneficial and economically viable
management of the world's forests.